Using Facebook®

Copyright © 2011 by Pearson Education, Inc.

ISBN-13: 978-0-7897-4524-8

ISBN-10: 0-7897-4524-0

Library of Congress Cataloging-in-Publication Data

Joshi, Kent.

  Using Facebook / Kent Joshi, Patrice-Anne Rutledge with Scott Morley.

    p. cm.

  ISBN-13: 978-0-7897-4524-8

  ISBN-10: 0-7897-4524-0

  1. Facebook (Electronic resource) 2. Online social networks. 3. Social networks—Computer network resources. 4. Web sites—Design. I. Rutledge, Patrice-Anne. II. Morley, Scott. III. Title.

  HM743.F33J67 2011

  006.7'54—dc22

                          2011004396

Printed in the United States of America

First Printing: May 2011

Trademarks

Warning and Disclaimer

Bulk Sales

Que Publishing offers excellent discounts on this book when ordered in quantity for bulk purchases or special sales. For more information, please contact

U.S. Corporate and Government Sales

1-800-382-3419

corpsales@pearsontechgroup.com

For sales outside of the U.S., please contact

International Sales

international@pearson.com

Associate Publisher
Greg Wiegand

Acquisitions Editor
Michelle Newcomb

Development Editor
Ginny Munroe

Managing Editor
Kristy Hart

Project Editor
Betsy Harris

Copy Editor
Geneil Breeze

Indexer
Brad Herriman

Proofreader
Kathy Ruiz

Technical Editor
Vince Averello

Publishing Coordinator
Cindy Teeters

Interior Designer
Anne Jones

Cover Designer
Anna Stingley

Compositor
Nonie Ratcliff

Contents at a Glance

Media Table of Contents

To register this product and gain access to the Free Web Edition and the audio and video files, go to **quepublishing.com/using**.

Table of Contents

About the Authors

Kent Joshi has helped others understand the ever-changing digital world as an author, consultant, and university lecturer for more than two decades. Recently, he developed and released several social media and Web 2.0 projects, which successfully included Facebook as part of a larger, online presence.

He enjoys writing, public speaking, and volunteering. He holds a Bachelor of Science degree from the University of Utah and is pursuing his master's degree at Harvard.

You can connect with him at www.facebook.com/AuthorKentJoshi.

Patrice-Anne Rutledge is the author of more than 30 books on business and technology, including *Using Facebook*, *Using LinkedIn*, and *The Truth About Profiting from Social Networking*, all from Pearson. As a social media expert, she is frequently quoted in major media outlets around the world, including CNN, Inc., Fox News, ABC News, MSN, and AOL.

Patrice is also the founder and principal of Pacific Ridge Media, a consulting and training firm that specializes in small business marketing, branding, and social media. You can learn more about Patrice's books and other projects on her author website (www.patricerutledge.com), her business website (www.pacificridgemedia.com), and her Facebook page (www.facebook.com/PacificRidgeMedia).

About the Contributor

Scott Morley has worked as an IT professional for more than 15 years, most recently as a Microsoft Architect.

Dedication

This book is dedicated to my Mom who taught me about living even when you have a grievous illness, and to my Dad who taught me about unconditional love.
—Kent Joshi

To my family, with thanks for their ongoing support and encouragement.
—Patrice-Anne Rutledge

Acknowledgments

First, I thank my incredible coauthor—Patrice-Anne Rutledge. Without her dedication and passion, this book would not exist.

Next, I want to thank Margie for her love and support as the book came together. Honey, I'm the lucky one.

I would also like to thank Michelle Newcomb for believing in the book and overseeing the entire process with heart and grace. I also want to thank all of Que's editorial team—it's no easy feat to keep up with a site that's constantly changing.

Finally, I thank Angel, our Australian cattle dog, for making sure food never goes unnoticed in our home. Someday you'll have to show me how you have more Facebook friends than I do.

If I have inadvertently left anyone out, please know I truly appreciate your work.

—Kent Joshi

Thanks to Michelle Newcomb, Ginny Munroe, Betsy Harris, Vince Averello, and Geneil Breeze for their feedback, suggestions, and attention to detail. And special thanks to my great coauthor on this book, Kent Joshi.

—Patrice-Anne Rutledge

We Want to Hear from You!

As the reader of this book, *you* are our most important critic and commentator. We value your opinion and want to know what we're doing right, what we could do better, what areas you'd like to see us publish in, and any other words of wisdom you're willing to pass our way.

As an associate publisher for Que Publishing, I welcome your comments. You can email or write me directly to let me know what you did or didn't like about this book—as well as what we can do to make our books better.

Please note that I cannot help you with technical problems related to the topic of this book. We do have a User Services group, however, where I will forward specific technical questions related to the book.

When you write, please be sure to include this book's title and author as well as your name, email address, and phone number. I will carefully review your comments and share them with the author and editors who worked on the book.

Email: feedback@quepublishing.com

Mail: Greg Wiegand
            Associate Publisher
            Que Publishing
            800 East 96th Street
            Indianapolis, IN 46240 USA

Reader Services

Visit our website and register this book at quepublishing.com/using for convenient access to any updates, downloads, or errata that might be available for this book.

Introduction

You may have heard about Facebook through a friend or on the news. With more than 500 million users, it's hard to ignore the talk about it. If you're ready to see what this social networking site is all about, but not sure where to begin, this book is for you.

The pages ahead are designed to quickly get you up to speed on Facebook. Plus, the companion online videos, podcasts (audio), and additional web content ensure you'll have the most up-to-date training given Facebook's changes.

So if you're ready, turn to Chapter 1, "An Introduction to Facebook," for a Facebook tour, or to the chapter of your choice, to get started.

Welcome to Facebook!

Who Is This Book For?

This book is for anyone who wants to use Facebook to

- Painlessly set up a Facebook account and add a profile picture
- Find people you've lost track of
- Communicate through messages, chats, and status updates
- Publish photos and videos
- Safeguard your personal information online
- Get mobile access to Facebook
- Attend or host an event
- Buy and sell items, browse for roommates, or find a job
- Promote your business, band, or brand
- Work with Facebook's applications

Using This Book

This book allows you to customize your own learning experience. The step-by-step instructions in the book give you a solid foundation in using Facebook, while rich and varied online content, including video tutorials and audio sidebars, provide the following:

- Demonstrations of step-by-step tasks covered in the book

- Additional tips or information on a topic

- Practical advice and suggestions

- Direction for more advanced tasks not covered in the book

Here's a quick look at a few structural features designed to help you get the most out of this book:

- **Chapter roadmaps:** At the beginning of each chapter is a list of the top-level topics addressed in that chapter. This list enables you to quickly see the information the chapter contains.

> **Notes** provide additional commentary or explanation that doesn't fit neatly into the surrounding text. Notes give detailed explanations of how something works, alternative ways of performing a task, and other tidbits to get you on your way.

- **Cross-references:** Many topics are connected to other topics in various ways. Cross-references help you link related information together, no matter where that information appears in the book. When another section is related to one you are reading, a cross-reference directs you to a specific page in the book on which you can find the related information.

 LET ME TRY IT tasks are presented in a step-by-step sequence so you can easily follow along.

 SHOW ME video walks through tasks you've just got to see—including bonus advanced techniques.

 TELL ME MORE audio delivers practical insights straight from the experts.

Special Features

More than just a book, your USING product integrates step-by-step video tutorials and valuable audio sidebars delivered through the **Free Web Edition** that comes with every USING book. For the price of the book, you get online access anywhere with a web connection—no books to carry, content is updated as the technology changes, and the benefit of video and audio learning.

About the USING Web Edition

The Web Edition of every USING book is powered by **Safari Books Online**, allowing you to access the video tutorials and valuable audio sidebars. Plus, you can search the contents of the book, highlight text and attach a note to that text, print your notes and highlights in a custom summary, and cut and paste directly from Safari Books Online.

To register this product and gain access to the Free Web Edition and the audio and video files, go to **quepublishing.com/using**.

This chapter describes what Facebook is, what it offers, and how its site pages are laid out.

1

An Introduction to Facebook

Facebook is a huge, online community. If you're familiar with the college "facebook" given at the beginning of a year so that you get to know your classmates, then you can imagine that facebook online. In a paper facebook, you see photos and biographies of your classmates. On Facebook, you see your friend's latest photos and videos with, at times, an extensive biography. You can write notes in your print facebook, but if you write notes on your friend's Facebook *Wall*, they and sometimes their friends will reply!

Facebook goes beyond the paper facebook by providing online tools for you to connect with virtually anyone on the site. You can look up old friends, chat and email with others, find and RVSP for events, shop for items, and find jobs. You can even connect to Facebook using your iPhone or another compatible mobile device.

Facebook also caters to business interests. Companies, bands, and celebrities promote on Facebook.

Finally, Facebook is well known for rapid changes. These updates, meant to keep Facebook fresh, useful, and competitive, sometimes result in frustration and confusion for both beginners and experts.

That's where this book comes in. It was written in early 2011 to help you get up to speed—and stay up to date through our updated online content—on one of the most popular yet constantly changing sites on the web.

Welcome to Facebook!

The Facebook Phenomenon

One way to describe the Facebook phenomenon is through people describing the valuable social connections made through the site:

"I left right after I graduated and haven't been back to my home state over the years. I often wondered what my classmates were up to, who was doing what, how does so and so look. How I wished I could hook back up with them. I got on

FB and have reconnected with my classmates, and it feels so good that FB allowed me to reconnect with people I spent the better part of my years growing up with. THANKS FB."

"My daughter died in a car crash two years ago. The day after she died a friend of hers set up a page in her memory. It helped us in our grief, and it was nice to be able to look at all the comments, memories, and photos that her friends posted. We even found out things about her personality that we didn't know before."

"When the earthquake destroyed part of the country, our girls were saved and taken to safety by a complete stranger who I found on Facebook. These girls were missing for over a month. I had no contact in that city and went to work making connections on Facebook with people around the world who were working there. I sent photos via Facebook, and I got a call saying the girls were found. They were sick, alone, hungry but ALIVE!"

—**From Facebook Stories**

You may have heard about Facebook starting as a site used by US college students. They would browse an online *facebook* or published biography with pictures of the student body to read about and contact each other.

Now, Facebook is a virtual world that's grown to hundreds of millions of users. Facebook Stories show one side of why people continue to use its network—for fun and potentially meaningful connections with like-minded people.

People are bringing parts of their lives online by connecting and sharing with family, friends, loved ones, and those with similar interests, businesses, or causes. Within this community, there are probably several potentially meaningful and valuable connections for you.

Of course, posting details of your life online can have a downside. Privacy is a concern for many people on Facebook. Chapter 6, "Safeguarding Your Information on Facebook," covers how to protect your Facebook information so it's not misused.

However, if you can't wait to sign up, you can get started immediately by reading Chapter 2, "Setting Up Your Facebook Account and Profile."

Facebook caters to personal and business interests. People use the website to keep in touch with friends and family, join groups, post pictures and videos, share music, chat, create events, submit comments to their profile from their mobile device, shop for goods, play games, develop applications, promote charities, and find jobs.

Despite all of these choices, the central theme for Facebook is finding and maintaining valuable social relationships. Here's a final Facebook Story with a perspective on the Facebook phenomena:

"When I was child, I made friends by becoming 'pen pals.' I'd write a letter, lick a stamp, and then wait for a reply. Sometimes another person would respond in place of who I wrote to! Now, I don't have to wait (and I know who's responding). I connect with from friends all over the world. Facebook has opened a whole new world to me as an author—the wonderful world of writers. Thanks, Facebook!"

A Tour of Facebook

Facebook uses a simple layout. After you have signed up (see Chapter 2), your Home page will begin to reflect your online interactions (see Figure 1.1). This page presents requests for you to consider, such as requests to "friend" someone, and lists your friends' activities in the News Feed.

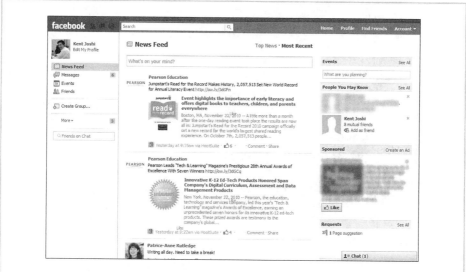

Figure 1.1   *A Home page on Facebook.*

Starting at the top of the page, you see Facebook's familiar blue banner pretty much wherever you explore to on the site. You use the Home option to navigate back to your Home page and Profile to see how your profile looks to others. The Find Friends option helps you find people you may know on the site, and Account accesses settings such as privacy. You can search the entire site using keywords in the Search box. Keep in mind Facebook rolls out changes in stages so you might not see exactly as it's mentioned here.

Along the left side are more options to view Messages or emails, scheduled Events, and information about your Friends. At the bottom, you see which friends are online to Chat.

Your Profile page is where you present yourself to everyone else on Facebook (see Figure 1.2). Your comments, photos, videos, and other digital interactions are captured here for your friends, family, significant other, business colleagues, and others depending on your privacy options.

Figure 1.2   *A Profile page on Facebook.*

In addition to the Home page options, you can share comments using your Wall, change your Info such as your birthday, and share Photos.

What Does Facebook Offer?

TELL ME MORE   Media 1.1—What You Can Do with Facebook
*Access this audio recording through your registered Web Edition at
my.safaribooksonline.com/9780132117029/media.*

Given Facebook is about social relationships, the site offers an extraordinary number of ways to connect with others.

Facebook is always adding more features, but here are some of the more popular ones:

- **Find your friends**—Probably the most often mentioned feature is the ability to locate and stay in touch with your friends, family, and loved ones no matter where they live. Yes, they can find you also. So, it's best to have your best foot or profile forward. Chapters 2, "Setting Up Your Facebook Account and Profile," and 3, "Finding and Adding Friends," help you set up a profile and locate your friends.

- **Make new friends and join groups**—Did I mention Facebook has hundreds of millions of users across the world? The chances are high to bump into and befriend someone or join a group that has similar interests as yours. There's a Facebook story of two people, with the same first and last name, who met on Facebook and later married! So even if you're not looking for an identically named life partner, you can read Chapters 3, "Finding and Adding Friends," and 10, "Joining and Creating Groups," to explore the rich opportunities to connect.

- **Find something to do**—You can search every public event on Facebook or narrow the results to the events your friends plan to attend. If you want to host your own get-together, Facebook only needs a few lines of information to advertise a public or private event of any size. The site also helps you manage the RVSPs. Chapter 11, "Joining and Creating Events," walks you through the details of events.

- **Express yourself (or your company, brand, or band)**—You can tell the Facebook community all about yourself through various digital vehicles including emails, posts, blogs, photos, videos, fan pages, virtual gifts, events, game playing outcomes, using your mobile device, and Facebook applications. Several chapters in the book get you started.

- **Peer into your children's or significant other's life**—If they are avid users, you can see a lot about who they are and how they represent themselves. Be warned that Facebook can be addicting. A family member of mine recently joined Facebook to connect with her daughter who spends a fair amount of time online. However, in a surreal turn of events, the daughter had to tell her mother that she had been on Facebook too long and to come to dinner. If you are concerned about what people can see you about you, Chapter 6, "Safeguarding Your Information on Facebook," can help you fine-tune the information that's publically available.

- **Shop for products or find an employment recruiter**—This is not as popular as the previous features, but it is growing. Facebook assumes you can make better purchasing decisions if you can read the seller's profile and see his friends. The same logic applies if you are looking for someone to represent you during your job hunt. You can find out more by reading Chapters 12, "Buying and Selling with Facebook Marketplace," and 14, "Making Business Connections on Facebook."

Hopefully this overview of Facebook's layout and popular features has sparked your curiosity to see more. You can get started by reading Chapter 2. If you already have a Facebook account and profile, you can read other chapters to learn how to get what you want from Facebook.

This chapter shows you everything you need to get started on Facebook including starting and personalizing your Facebook profile and updating your private account information.

2

Setting Up Your Facebook Account and Profile

Joining Facebook

Facebook's requirements to join are straightforward. You have to be at least 13 years old and have a working email address. That's it. As for cost, Facebook is free.

Facebook first asks you to create an account and then a profile. Your account stores private information such as your password. Your profile shares all the information you want to publicize.

It's best to be completely truthful when you describe yourself during the steps to create your account and profile. If Facebook's thorough checking of your account doesn't reject the name "Superman," chances are your colleagues and old classmates on Facebook may reject communications from nicknames they don't recognize. You can always add details to your profile later.

Signing Up

Given you meet Facebook's easy criteria, your first step is register for a Facebook account. If you're not a Facebook user, you need an account to log in.

The sign-up process has two parts. First, you provide basic information to obtain an ID and password. This first part is mandatory. The second part involves finding others you may know on Facebook and the option to post your photo. The second part is optional and can be filled in later.

If Facebook's sign-up steps don't match what you see in the next section, check out this book's online screencasts. These are revised whenever Facebook rolls out a major update.

LET ME TRY IT

Sign Up for a Facebook Account

When you sign up for Facebook, you need to complete all the fields on Facebook's sign-up form. Follow these steps to sign up for an account:

1. In your web browser, type **www.facebook.com**. The sign-up form displays (see Figure 2.1).

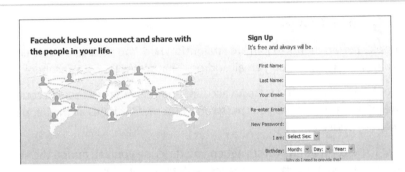

Figure 2.1   *Facebook's sign-up form to get an account.*

If you're a Windows user, you can use Internet Explorer. If you're using a Mac, use Safari.

2. In the First Name and Last Name fields, type your first name and last name.

Do not use nicknames. You can change your name, for example, from a married to a maiden name later to make it easier for people to find you.

3. In the Your Email field, provide a working email address. Facebook will email you at this address to confirm and fully activate your account. Repeat your email address in the Re-enter Email field.

4. In the New Password field, choose a password that is six characters or longer.

5. In the I am field, select your gender.

6. For the Birthday field, select the Month, Day, and Year from the drop-down lists. Again, you need to be at least 13 years old to join.

7. If you're satisfied with the information you've typed, click Sign Up.

8. When you see the Security Check screen, type the words that are displayed. Currently, the security check is not case sensitive. Typing "Aspen" or "aspen" registers as the same word.

9. When you're satisfied with security word(s) and agree to Facebook's Terms of Use and Privacy Policy, click Sign Up.

> Did you really read the fine print when signing up? Most people don't, but you're encouraged to do so. The Privacy policy describes how Facebook might use your personal information and provides a helpful summary. Facebook's Terms of Service, also called Rights and Responsibilities, goes over the do's and dont's to keep your profile from being suspended. You can read more by searching in Help located in the lower-right corner of most Facebook screens.

10. Select skip this step if you see one of these Getting Started screens (see Figure 2.2 or Figure 2.3). If you don't see either screen, go to step 11.

Figure 2.2 *Skip the Getting Started screen to find your friends on Facebook using your email address.*

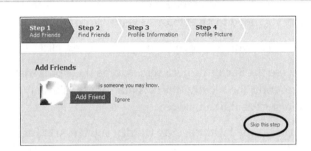

Figure 2.3   *Skip the Getting Started screen where Facebook shows a potential friend.*

11. If you do not see a Getting Started screen, you will see a note from Facebook asking you to confirm your email address. Open your email program as you normally do, open the email from Facebook, and click on the confirmation link (see Figure 2.4). You may also receive a confirmation code through email that you'll enter into Facebook. Either way, you'll officially confirm your account (see Figure 2.5).

Figure 2.4   *Facebook emailed a confirmation link.*

Figure 2.5   *Facebook confirmed your account.*

Congratulations! You can now tell friends and family you've joined Facebook! If you log out now, you can log back in with your account information, which is your email and Facebook password. Let's discuss completing the sign-up process.

 **LET ME TRY IT**

Complete the Registration Process

After you complete the final steps in registration, you are asked to search for friends on Facebook and post a photo of yourself. These getting started steps are optional. You can certainly provide all requested information on the spot, but we are choosing to skip these steps instead. You can complete them later.

1. If you aren't already signed into Facebook, log in now. To do so, type **www. facebook.com** into your web browser, fill in your email and Facebook password, and click Login (see Figure 2.6).

Figure 2.6   *To log in, type in your email and Facebook password, and click Login.*

2. In the next screen, Facebook might display someone you already know (see Figure 2.3). For now, select Skip This Step to take no action. You can add them as a friend later by reading Chapter 3, "Finding and Adding Friends." We are skipping this step to complete registration.

3. When asked to find your friends by searching your email account, select Skip This Step to take no action (see Figure 2.2). We search for friends in Chapter 3.

4. When asked to provide schooling and work information, select Skip to take no action (see Figure 2.7). You will add these later.

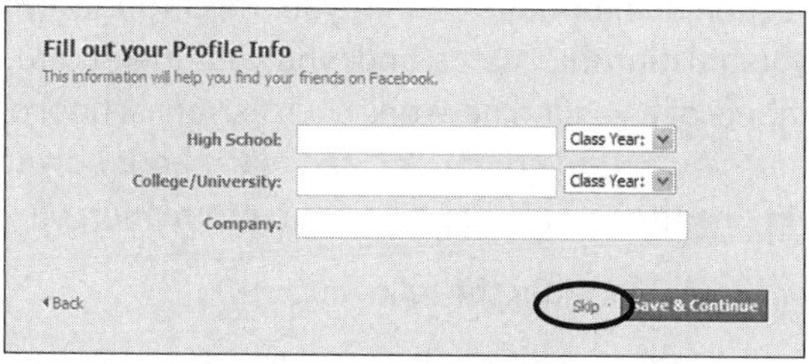

Fill out your Profile Info
This information will help you find your friends on Facebook.

High School:		Class Year:
College/University:		Class Year:
Company:		

◀ Back   Skip   Save & Continue

Figure 2.7   *Skip the step to find friends using your prior education and employers.*

5. When asked to provide your picture, select Skip to take no action (see Figure 2.8). You will add it later.

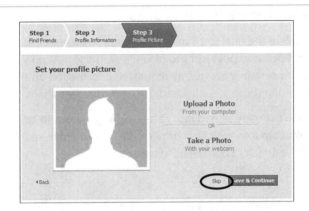

Figure 2.8   *Skip the step to send your digital photo to Facebook.*

You've completed the registration process. Now, you can begin exploring Facebook and adding to your profile.

Personalizing Your Profile

Assuming you've signed up and finished registration, you have the freedom to experience everything Facebook has to offer. You should start adding to your newly created profile.

 TELL ME MORE   Media 2.1—Personalizing Your Profile
Access this audio recording through your registered Web Edition at
my.safaribooksonline.com/9780132117029/media.

A *profile* is a collection of information about you. This includes what you enjoy in your free time, your relationship status, and who your friends are. Your Facebook friends and members of a verified network, such as your school or work, can see these details unless you exclude them. You can read about how to exclude some Facebook users in Chapter 6, "Safeguarding Your Information on Facebook."

To build out your profile, consider the following:

- **What are you looking for from Facebook?**—Do you want a profile to connect with friends and family, find a job, or promote a cause? You get the best results when you know what you want.

- **What's your comfort level for privacy?**—You can hide personal information while still making it easy for others to find and connect with you. For example, you can limit who can see you in Facebook search results to just friends or friends of friends.

Do you want to represent a band, product, non-profit organization, or celebrity status? A Facebook "page" might be a better approach than a profile. On the Facebook Sign Up form, click Create a Page for a Celebrity, Band, or Business and select Click Here to sign up. You can learn more about using Facebook for business purposes in Chapter 14, "Making Business Connections on Facebook."

You now have a good blueprint to put together your profile. Here's a list of all profile sections. Each of these is optional to complete, but you'll find some are pretty useful in the long run if you take the time to them fill out.

Keep in mind that Facebook summarizes all the following information, including contact information such as your street address, on your profile's main page.

- **Your Profile Picture**—A picture of yourself so others recognize it's you.

- **Tagged Photos**—Under your name, Facebook shows a row of the five most recent photos you were identified or *tagged* in. Tagging is useful to find you in a group photo. In this chapter, we'll just work with your profile picture, so if you want to change your tagged photo list or albums, you can find out how by reading Chapter 7, "Publishing Photos."

- **Basic Information**—This section asks for general information such as your gender, birthday, and current city. This is also where you'll find the box called "About Me" which asks for a few sentences about yourself.

- **Featured People**—This is the relationship section where you describe your relationship status, such as married, and link to your significant other's profile. You can also list immediate family members and link to their profiles. Your Facebook friends are found here to categorize into groups, called friend lists, for activities such as hiking and to "feature" specific friends in your profile page. Finally, there's a *Friendship Page* which is a like a profile and shows shared content between two people. You'll see your mutual friends, common things you like, comments made to each other, mutual events, and more. You can read more about this in Chapter 5, "Keeping Up to Date with Your Friends."

- **Education and Work**—Your academic and career information, plus the names of people who worked or attended class with you, can be listed here.

- **Banner**—A banner appears under your name and summarizes certain fields from the basic information, education and work history, and featured people categories.

- **Philosophy**—Your religious and political views, people you find inspirational, and your favorite quotations can be added here.

- **Arts and Entertainment**—Want to share your favorite music, book, movie, or TV show? You can by capture that information here.

- **Sports**—This has fields for the sports you play, your favorite teams, and your favorite athletes.

- **Activities and Interests**—This section broadly captures your hobbies and interests.

- **Contact Information**—You can provide your electronic—email, Instant Messenger (IM), and websites associated with you—and physical—phone and street address—means to find you.

It is recommended that you wait to fill out the Contact Information section unless you are familiar with Facebook's privacy options. Despite Facebook's updates to privacy, some settings default to the least restrictive. This means everyone on the Internet can see this information in your profile.

Because friends and family typically know how to reach you, your Facebook experience isn't diminished by leaving this blank. However, you're free to complete this section and restrict who can see it using Facebook's privacy controls described briefly in this chapter and in more detail in Chapter 6.

As mentioned before, it's optional for you to complete these suggested sections. If you choose not to, you will have a bare-bones profile with workable functionality. However, to connect with others and see what Facebook is all about, it's suggested you post information to your profile that you are comfortable sharing. You are free to restrict the right to view profile information, except for the following: your name, gender, profile photo, networks, and username. These are always set for *Everyone* on the Internet to view. Facebook does this so friends can find and recognize it's really you. Now, some of these options are visible in an indirect way. For example, if you choose to hide your gender when others view your profile, no one will see it when they directly view your profile. However, Facebook can indirectly present your gender through actions such as profile changes. As an example, "Kent added State University to his education" may display even if your gender is hidden.

After joining Facebook and filling in your profile, it's not uncommon to get deluged with Friend requests. You may hear from work colleagues, old classmates, and friends of friends. You can refer to Chapter 3 to handle requests if they start pouring in.

Now that you have an idea of the sections you want to fill out, simply go through the steps in the following sections to do so.

Add a Profile Picture

Though adding a picture to your profile is optional, most people do. You need a digital photo or a built-in camera on your computer. You should use a portrait picture so people recognize you. If you decide to instead to use a family or other similar group shot, be sure it's easy for others to find you in the group. Also, your profile photo defaults to viewable by everyone on the Internet. This ensures people recognize you, so choose your photo with this wide audience in mind.

 SHOW ME Media 2.2—Add a Profile Photo
Access this video file through your registered Web Edition at
my.safaribooksonline.com/9780132117029/media.

 LET ME TRY IT

Add a Profile Picture

The following steps show you how to add a photo to your profile from your computer's drive:

1. If needed, log in to Facebook. To log in, type **www.facebook.com** into your web browser, fill in your email address and Facebook password, and click Login.

2. Select Profile in the upper right (see Figure 2.9).

Figure 2.9 *Select Profile to go to your Profile page.*

3. Select Edit Profile in the upper right (see Figure 2.10).

4. Select Profile Picture in the upper left (see Figure 2.11).

Figure 2.10   *Select Edit Profile to bring up the Profile menu.*

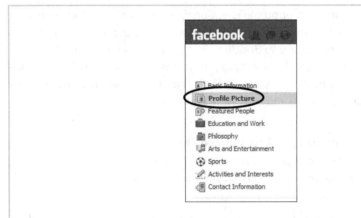

Figure 2.11   *Select Profile Picture from the menu on the left.*

5. To open a new window to find and choose your photo file, select Browse (see Figure 2.12).

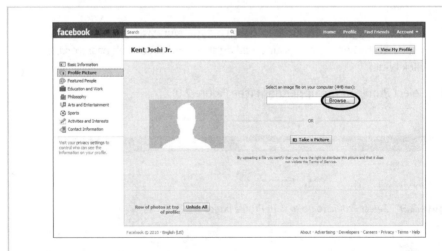

Figure 2.12   *Select Browse to open a window to choose the file containing your profile picture.*

Your photo file must be 4 megabytes (MB) in size or smaller. It also cannot violate the Terms of Service. This means your photo cannot be illegal, such as copyrighted, or considered immoral by Facebook.

6. After you locate your photo file, double-click the file or select Open to send it to Facebook (see Figure 2.13).

Figure 2.13   *Double-click your photo file to send it to Facebook.*

7. If your photo doesn't display, you might need to refresh your Internet browser.

8. To see your changes on the profile page, select View My Profile (see Figure 2.14).

Add Basic Information

The Basic Information category asks for fairly basic information. As with all profile categories, none of the fields are mandatory. Because a summary of this information appears on your profile page so friends recognize you, you might want to start with entering your current city and updating how your birthday is displayed.

  SHOW ME   Media 2.3—Add Basic Information
Access this video file through your registered Web Edition at
my.safaribooksonline.com/9780132117029/media.

Figure 2.14   *Select View My Profile to view your profile with your changes.*

 LET ME TRY IT

Add Basic Information

The following steps show you how to complete the Basic Information section of your profile. It's a quick way to provide introductory information about you.

1. Assuming you are logged in, select Profile from the blue menu bar in the upper right (see Figure 2.15).

Figure 2.15   *Select Profile to go to your Profile page.*

2. Select Edit Profile in the upper right (see Figure 2.16). The screen defaults to the Basic Information category.

3. When you start typing in a field, Facebook may suggest potential matches. Select one of them to use it in your profile (see Figure 2.17).

4. Complete as many fields you want using the following list as a guide:

   - **Current City**—The city you live in. This helps friends find you and for you to find events on Facebook near you.

Figure 2.16   *Select Edit Profile to bring up the Profile menu.*

Figure 2.17   *Suggested names for Current City.*

- **Hometown**—Your birth city or the city where you grew up.

- **Gender**—With this selected, Facebook personalizes your comments with "John changed his Quotations" instead of "John changed their Quotations." You can hide if you're male or female by unchecking the box titled Show My Sex in My Profile.

- **Birthday**—With this typed in, Friends get notified of your birthday. You can change how your birthday displays on your profile page by using the drop-down menu next to the field (see Figure 2.18).

Figure 2.18   *Change how your birthday displays on the profile page using the drop-down menu.*

- **Interested In: Women/Men**—This field can have different interpretations to the Facebook community. For some, this may mean an innocent interest for a friendship or platonic activity, but to others, it can describe sexual orientation. With that mind, you can choose none, one, or both options.

- **Languages**—To add multiple entries, type the language and select it from the list.

- **About Me**—This box usually contains a brief description of who you are, what you do, and maybe a personal motto. If you are typing in your first draft, don't stress over perfection. You can add some detail now and refine it later.

5. Click Save Changes at the bottom of the screen when you have filled in your desired fields (see Figure 2.19).

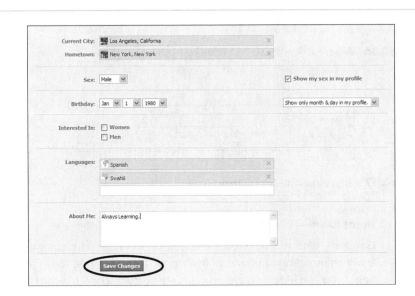

Figure 2.19   *Select Save Changes when you have filled in your desired Basic Information fields.*

Add Featured People

The Featured People category captures your relationship status and family tree. All fields are optional to fill out, but you might find it worthwhile to add some information as it makes it easier to stay in touch and even organize get-togethers. Any filled-in information is summarized on your profile page.

 SHOW ME   Media 2.4—Add Featured People
Access this video file through your registered Web Edition at
my.safaribooksonline.com/9780132117029/media.

 LET ME TRY IT

Add Featured People

These steps show you how to link to your friends and family online. They also show you how to organize your friends into lists.

1. Assuming you have logged in, select Profile from the blue menu bar in the upper right.

2. Select the Edit Profile button in the upper right, under the menu bar.

3. Select Featured People from menu on the left (see Figure 2.20).

Figure 2.20   *Select Featured People from the menu on the left.*

4. Complete as many fields you want using the following list as a guide:

   - **Relationship Status**—Select your status from the drop-down menu (see Figure 2.21). Keep in mind, some choices can have several meanings to the Facebook community—for example, It's Complicated and In an Open Relationship. If you are in a relationship with someone else, you can link to that person's profile by typing his or her name in the With field. He or she needs a Facebook account, must be a friend, and needs to accept your request to be in a relationship (see Figure 2.22).

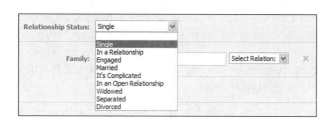

Figure 2.21   *Choose your relationship status from the menu.*

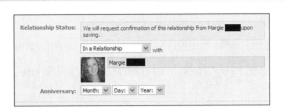

Figure 2.22   *Link to your significant other's profile.*

- **Family**—You can list a family member name and link to his or her profile by typing his or her name and selecting the relationship—for example, son. The family member needs a Facebook account, must be a friend, and needs to accept your request (see Figure 2.23). Add additional family members by selecting Add Another Family Member below family name field and repeat this step.

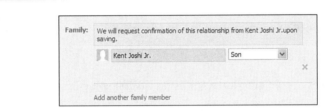

Figure 2.23   *Link to a family member's profile or add another family member.*

- **Featured Friends**—You can call out certain friends (best man, hiking buddies) or family members (The Smiths) by using a friend list. Facebook friends are automatically added to a friend list called Friends and linked family members are automatically made part of a friend list called Family. When you feature a friend list, it appears on the left side of your profile. A friend list is useful to organize groups of friends, allow other friends to understand what makes this group of friends special, and customize privacy. For example, you can set privacy settings for family vacation photos so only those in the "Family" friend list can view it. The next four steps apply to Featured Friends.

5. To create and feature a new friend list, select Create New List (see Figure 2.24).

6. Type in a new list name, choose your friends, and select Create List to save it (see Figure 2.25).

Figure 2.24   *Select create new list to create a friend list.*

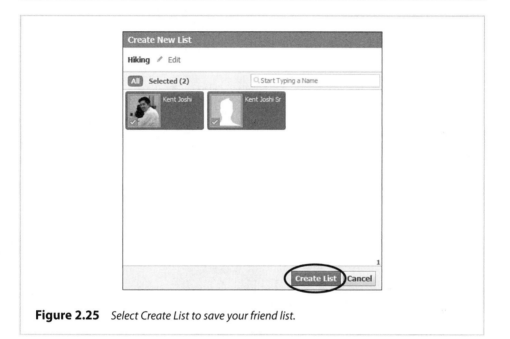

Figure 2.25   *Select Create List to save your friend list.*

7. To feature an existing friend list, select Add an Existing List or Group (see Figure 2.26).

Figure 2.26   *Select Add an Existing List or Group to feature an existing friend list.*

8. Select the desired friend list and then select Add (see Figure 2.27).

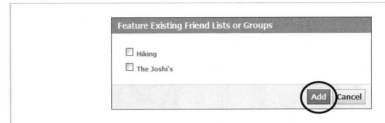

Figure 2.27   *Select the existing friend list or group you want to feature and then select Add.*

A friend or group list must have least one member to be featured. To add members, select Account from the blue menu bar in the upper right and then Edit Friends.

9. Click Save Changes at the bottom of the screen when you have filled in your desired fields (see Figure 2.28).

Figure 2.28   *Select Save Changes when you have filled in your desired Featured Relationship fields.*

Add Education and Work Information

The Education and Work Information category not only captures where you worked or went to school but also the names of who you worked or went to class with. As with all profile categories, filling this out is optional. However, if you take the time to type in entries, it becomes easier for your former classmates and colleagues to find you, and the information will be summarized on your profile page.

 SHOW ME Media 2.5—Add Education and Work
Access this video file through your registered Web Edition at
my.safaribooksonline.com/9780132117029/media.

 LET ME TRY IT

Add Education and Work Information

The following directions show how to add education and work information to your profile. If you your colleagues or classmates are also Facebook friends, these steps show how to link to their profiles.

1. Assuming you have logged in, select Profile from the blue menu bar in the upper right.

2. Select the Edit Profile button in the upper right, under the menu bar.

3. Select Education and Work from menu on the left (see Figure 2.29).

4. To add work information, type a company name in the Employer field and fill in as many of these additional fields as you want to create a job entry:

   - **Position, City/Town, Time Period**—Type the position you held, the city where it was located, and the time period you held it. If you uncheck I Currently Work Here, you can fill out the date you left this employer.

   - **With**—Type the name of a coworker who's a Facebook friend.

   - **Description**—You can type that the job was an internship or some other information that would be useful to others to identify this.

5. To save your job information, select Add Job (see Figure 2.30).

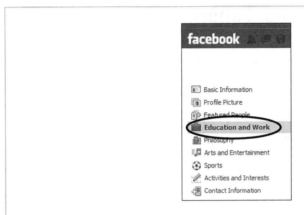

Figure 2.29   *Select Education and Work from the menu on the left.*

Figure 2.30   *Select Add Job to save your entry.*

6. To add a project within a job, select Add a Project (see Figure 2.31). Fill in as many of these optional fields as you want to create a project entry:

    - **Project, Time Period**—Type the project name and the beginning to ending dates you worked on it. If you check I Am Currently on This Project, you only need to complete the date you started on the project.

    - **With**—Type the name of a coworker who's a Facebook friend.

    - **Description**—You can type that the project position was an internship or other additional details.

7. To save your job information, select Add Project (see Figure 2.32).

Figure 2.31   *Select Add a Project to add a project within a job.*

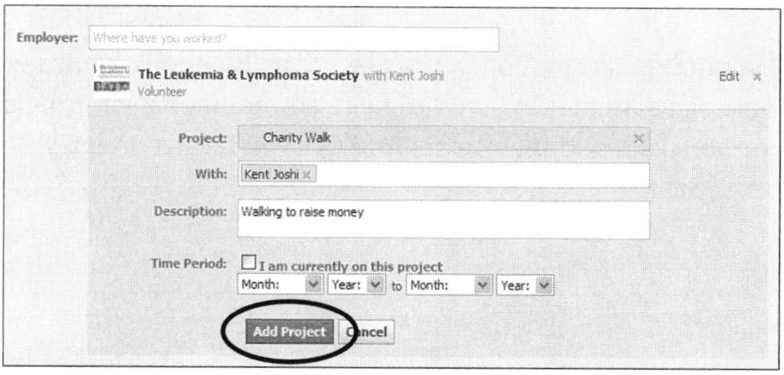

Figure 2.32   *Select Add Project to save your entry.*

8. To add College/University information, type your school information, Facebook friends who were classmates in the With field, your fields or majors in the Concentration field, whether you attended for College/Graduate School, and then select Add School to save (see Figure 2.33).

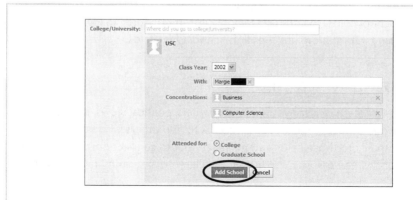

Figure 2.33   *Select Add School to save your entry.*

9. To add a class, select Add a Class under the College/University entry (see Figure 2.34)

Figure 2.34   *Select Add a Class to add a class within a College or University entry.*

10. Type your class information in the Class field, Facebook friends who were teachers or classmates in the With field, any additional information in the Description field, and then select Add Class to save your entry (see Figure 2.35).

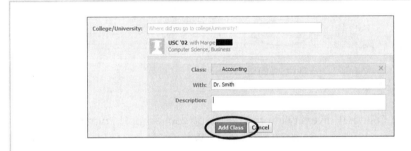

Figure 2.35   *Select Add Class to save your entry.*

11. To add High School information, follow step 8 by typing information into the High School fields. To add High School class information, follow steps 9 and 10, typing information into the High School Class fields.

Add Philosophy Information

The philosophy category is for your religious beliefs, political views, inspirations, and favorite quotations. If you joined Facebook to find others who share your views, you can fill out those fields and make it easier to connect online. As with all profile categories, any optional fields that are filled out are summarized on your profile page.

 **LET ME TRY IT**

Add Philosophy

You can add information about your philosophy by following these steps. One section, People Who Inspire You, displays a Facebook profile if it exists.

1. Assuming you have logged in, select Profile from the blue menu bar in the upper right.

2. Select the Edit Profile button in the upper right, under the menu bar.

3. Select Philosophy from menu on the left (see Figure 2.36).

Figure 2.36   *Select Philosophy from the menu on the left.*

4. Complete as many fields as you want. You can add more entries to the People Who Inspire You field by typing a new entry and then selecting a suggested match. Click Save Changes at the bottom when you're done (see Figure 2.37).

As you begin typing, Facebook suggests a match. The suggestions tie to the profile field. For example, only political affiliations are suggested when you type in the Political View field.

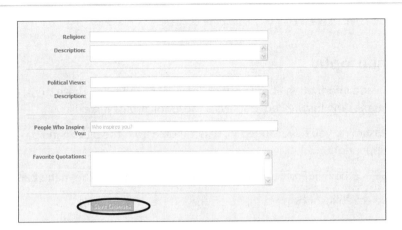

Figure 2.37 *Complete as many Philosophy fields as you want and then select Save Changes.*

Add Your Favorite Arts and Entertainment

In each of the Arts and Entertainment sections, you can list multiple choices. The sections are favorite music type, book, movie, TV show, and game. Similar to Philosophy fields, Facebook suggests matches based on the field and what you type. For example, only books are suggested when you type titles in the Books field. All the fields are optional to complete. A summary of your favorite selections are presented on your profile page.

 LET ME TRY IT

Add Arts and Entertainment

These steps demonstrate how to enter information into the Arts and Entertainment section of your profile. Similar to other profile sections, you can link certain categories to existing Facebook profiles.

1. Assuming you have logged in, select Profile from the blue menu bar in the upper right.

2. Select the Edit Profile button in the upper right, under the menu bar.

3. Select Arts and Entertainment from menu on the left (see Figure 2.38).

4. Complete as many fields you want (see Figure 2.39) and then click Save Changes at the bottom when you're done. You can add multiple entries by typing a new entry and selecting a suggested match.

Figure 2.38   *Select Arts and Entertainment from the menu on the left.*

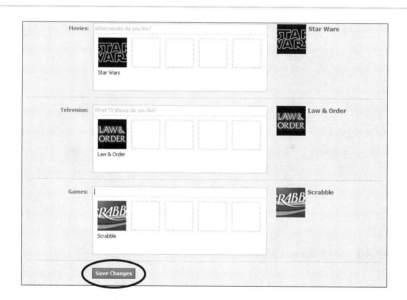

Figure 2.39   *Complete as many Arts and Entertainment fields as you want and then select Save Changes.*

Add Sports Information

You can list several of your favorite sports teams and favorite athletes. In the Sports You Play field, you have the option to include friend's profiles who play that sport with you. It's another way to connect on Facebook. As with other profile categories, Facebook suggests matches based on the field name and what you type. For example, names are suggested when you type an athlete's name in Favorite Athletes. All fields in the Sports category are optional to fill out, but any you choose to complete are summarized on your profile page.

 LET ME TRY IT

Add Sports

This section section takes you through entering in your favorite sports to watch and play. You can link your entries to Facebook profiles if they exist.

1. Assuming you have logged in, select Profile from the blue menu bar in the upper right.

2. Select the Edit Profile button in the upper right, under the menu bar.

3. Select Sports from menu on the left (see Figure 2.40).

Figure 2.40 *Select Sports from the menu on the left.*

4. In the Sports You Play field, type the sport's name. In the With field, type the names of any Facebook friends who participate in the sport with you. Select Add Sport to save your entry (see Figure 2.41).

5. In Favorite Teams and Favorite Athletes, type and select your entry. Select the appropriate Save Changes button when you're done (see Figure 2.42).

Figure 2.41 *Select Add Sport to save your entry.*

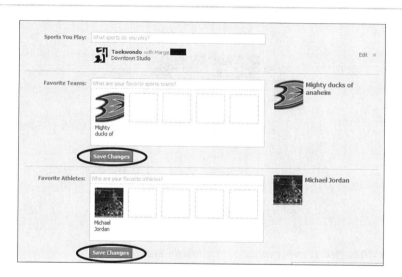

Figure 2.42 *Complete as many Sports fields as you want and then select Save Changes.*

Add Activities and Interests

The Activities and Interests category is another way to connect to other Facebook users. Activities are mainly pursuits with which you can list other Facebook friends who enjoy that activity with you. Interests can be the same as Activities but are mainly meant for individual pursuits because you can't link them to another Facebook friend. For example, you may hike as an activity with Jane but enjoy studying the history of a hiking area as an interest. Facebook suggests matches based on the field name and what you type. Both fields in this category are optional to fill out, but any you choose to complete are summarized on your profile page.

 **LET ME TRY IT**

Add Activities and Interests

Follow these steps to capture your activities and interests on Facebook. It's a fun way to share your mutual interests and activities with others.

1. Assuming you have logged in, select Profile from the blue menu bar in the upper right.

2. Select the Edit Profile button in the upper right, under the menu bar.

3. Select Activities and Interests from menu on the left (see Figure 2.43).

Figure 2.43   *Select Activities and Interests from the menu on the left.*

4. Complete as many fields you want. You can add multiple Interests and Activities. Type your information and select a suggested match. For Activities, you can link one to a Facebook friend by typing and selecting the friend's name from the list (see Figure 2.44). Select Add Activity to save the entry.

5. When you are done entering your activities and interests, select Save Changes at the bottom (see Figure 2.45).

Figure 2.44   *Type and select a friend's name from the list to link him or her to an activity.*

Figure 2.45   *Complete as many Activities and Interests fields as you want and then select Save Changes.*

If you want to find a list of sites you "liked," select Profile, Activities and Interests, and then Show Other Pages at the bottom of the page (see Figure 2.45).

Add Contact Information

As mentioned earlier, be cautious and use common sense when providing your contact information to a website with more than 500 million active users. Profile information, through Facebook's initially loose privacy settings or deliberate hacking, does get released. All contact information fields are summarized on the profile page. You can restrict what visitors see using privacy settings. To read more about managing your privacy, see Chapter 6.

 **LET ME TRY IT**

Add Contact Information

This section guides you through the many fields in Contact Information. It also covers how to add a Facebook Badge to your website.

1. Assuming you have logged in, select Profile from the blue menu bar in the upper right.

2. Select the Edit Profile button in the upper right, under the menu bar.

3. Select Contact Information from menu on the left (see Figure 2.46).

Figure 2.46 *Select Contact Information from the menu on the left.*

4. Complete as many fields you want using the following list as a guide:

   • **Emails**—Select Add/Remove Emails to add more addresses or change your existing one. This controls the emails Facebook uses to contact you.

   • **IM Screen Names**—Add your screen name for your favorite messaging tool. Visitors to your profile see if you are connected through any of the tools listed in the drop-down menu.

   • **Mobile, Other Phone**—Enter your phone numbers and be sure to select your country for the right international dialing code. This information is optional and shows on your profile page, so use common sense if you decide to post.

- **Address, City/Town, Zip, Neighborhood**—Enter your physical or mailing address if you are comfortable posting this optional information online. It displays on your profile page depending on your privacy settings.

- **Website**—Add websites you want to show on your profile page. You don't need to include "http://." You can add more than one site by separating each one with commas (,) or semicolons (;) or by putting each site address on a new line.

5. Select Save Changes when you're done (see Figure 2.47).

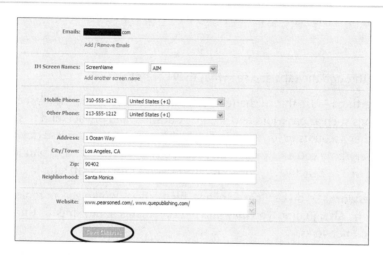

Figure 2.47   *Complete as many Contact Information fields as you want and then select Save Changes.*

Speaking of websites, you can add a Facebook Badge to one. A badge is a clickable image composed of selected profile information, called items, and Facebook's logo. Some examples of items you can add to your badge are your profile picture or a site you like. To create a badge, select the Add a Badge to Your Site link at the bottom of your profile page. After you choose and configure the badge you want, Facebook adds the badge if your site uses a supported platform such as Blogger. You can also manually add the badge by copying a little HTML code provided by Facebook to your site. As always, take precautions when publicizing personal information in a badge to a website. For more information and tips, see www.facebook.com/badges.

Managing and Downloading Your Account Information

Your account information, called My Account, controls information considered private and generally not part of your Facebook profile. This includes your password, payment information, when you last logged in, and other items.

It's recommended you change your privacy settings from the default of the least restrictive permissions as it affects how some of your account information is handled. This is not covered here, but you can read more about this in Chapter 6.

Let's go through the tabs and see what they control:

- **Settings**—Use this to change your real name, username, email, security settings such as password and security question, and privacy, and to set up other accounts to log in (called Linked Accounts). You can also download everything you ever posted on Facebook such as photos and phone numbers as well as deactivate your account. We'll dive into this tab later in this chapter.

- **Networks**—You can join a college, high school, workplace, or regional network. After joining, you may find old classmates or new friends through common networks.

- **Notifications**—You can choose an email or mobile phone notification whenever something happens on Facebook that involves you. It's an extensive list, but some examples are whenever someone adds you as a friend, posts on your wall, or invites you to an event.

- **Mobile**—To use your cell phone to interact with Facebook, you need to activate Facebook Mobile with this option. Once set up, you can update your status and upload photos from your phone. You can read more about this in Chapter 9, "Your Mobile Access to Facebook."

- **Language**—You can change the primary language used on Facebook.

- **Payments**—Facebook Credits are the "currency" to pay for virtual gifts, play games, and post Facebook Ads. You purchase Credits using your credit card or a gift card. Use this setting to manage Credits and how you pay for them.

- **Facebook Ads**—You can control how Facebook uses your information to show in ads and applications to your friends. For example, did you select "like" for a sushi restaurant advertisement? If so, your friends may get that ad with your name "liking" it. You can change your settings so your information appears to friends only or to no one.

If you'd like to change options under the Settings tab, simply go through the steps in the following section.

LET ME TRY IT

Change Your Settings under My Account

You can change the settings for your account by performing the following general steps. These settings control information considered private by Facebook.

1. Assuming you have logged in, select Account and then Account Settings from the blue menu bar in the upper right (see Figure 2.48).

Figure 2.48   *Select Account, then Account Settings.*

2. Make the change you want by selecting one or more of the following settings (see Figure 2.49):

   - **Name**—You can change your real name.
   - **Username**—You can create a friendly URL or *Username* as it's called in Facebook. It makes it easier for others to get to your profile. For example, http://www.facebook.com/authorkentjoshi can replace http://www.facebook.com/profile.php?id=1234.
   - **Email**—You can change your email address that Facebook uses to contact you.
   - **Password**—You can change the password you use to login to Facebook.
   - **Linked Accounts**—You can automatically log into Facebook whenever you log into another linked account.

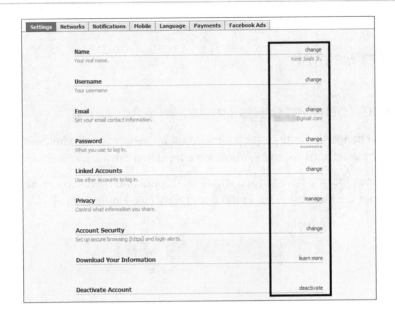

Figure 2.49   *Select the link to the right of the setting you want to change.*

- **Privacy**—You can manage your privacy settings. These options control information friends can use to find you on Facebook, who can see what you share on Facebook, and how to block people and applications. To learn more, see Chapter 6.

- **Account Security**—You can get an email or text message if an unregistered PC or mobile device logs into your account. You can also see when your account was last active. To learn more, see Chapters 6 and 9.

- **Download Your Information**—You can get a copy of everything you've shared on Facebook including all correspondence with friends. This may help if the only copy of a photo or phone number is on Facebook.

- **Deactivate Account**—You can temporarily disable your Profile and remove your information from anything you've shared on Facebook. You can reactivate it later and everything will be restored back to where you left it. This is not the same as deleting your account, which purges it from Facebook with no chance for recovery.

This chapter helps you find and add friends, including your email contacts, coworkers, and classmates.

3

Finding and Adding Friends

Facebook makes it easy for you to find and add friends. You can add your email contacts, coworkers, and classmates with the help of automated tools, search all Facebook users for potential friends, and invite people who aren't on Facebook yet to join. Facebook even suggests potential friends for you, based on the data you enter on the site and your existing friendships.

In this chapter, you explore the many ways to develop your Facebook network of friends. You can also listen to tips on finding and adding friends and watch videos that show you how to add your web email contacts as friends, add your coworkers as friends, upload a contact file, and accept friend requests.

Finding and Adding Friends on Facebook

As a new Facebook user, the fastest way to grow your network is to add your real-life friends as Facebook friends. Fortunately, Facebook simplifies the process of finding and adding your existing email contacts, coworkers, and classmates. During the initial sign-up process, Facebook prompts you to search for your friends. If you completed this step, you should already have made some progress in building your network. If you decided to skip this step, you can start the process now.

 TELL ME MORE Media 3.1—Ways to Find and Add Friends on Facebook

Access this audio recording through your registered Web Edition at
my.safaribooksonline.com/9780132117029/media.

Facebook offers a variety of ways to find and connect with your existing friends. You can

- Enter your email address in the Search Your Email for Friends Already on Facebook section on the Welcome to Facebook page. This page displays when you log in to Facebook as a new user. If you've been using Facebook for a while, you won't see this page.

- Click the Find Friends link in the upper-right corner of the Facebook screen to open the Friends page where you can search for email contacts, coworkers, and classmates.

- Review the options in the Find More Friends and Get Connected sections on the right side of the Facebook page. The content in these sections is personalized based on your past experience with Facebook.

- On the left menu of your Home page, click the Friends link. Then, click the Find Friends link that appears below it. This also opens the Friends page.

- Go to www.facebook.com/friends while logged in to Facebook. This opens the Find Friends page, which is nearly identical to the Friends page.

- Review the people suggested in the People You May Know section on the right side of the Facebook page. If you see someone you know, click the Add as Friend link to send a friend request. You can also click the See All link to view a longer list of people Facebook thinks you might know, based on an analysis of your current friends and information you entered about your employment and education.

Although having many options is a good thing, it can also lead to confusion. The rest of this section provides step-by-step instructions on the most popular ways to add friends.

Be aware that because the content Facebook displays on your page is dynamic and personalized based on your previous activity on the site, all these options might not be available to you or might appear in a different format. For example, what you see as a new user might differ from the options available to a long-time Facebook user who needs less help with the site.

Connecting with Your Web Email Contacts

One of the fastest ways to start building your Facebook network is to import your web email contacts from email services such as Windows Live Hotmail, Yahoo! Mail, Gmail, AOL, MSN, Sbcglobal.net, Verizon.net, Comcast, and others. You can also import your Skype contacts.

If you use Microsoft Outlook, Mozilla Thunderbird, Apple Mail, or some other desktop email application, see "Connecting with Your Desktop Email Contacts on Facebook" later in this chapter for more information.

SHOW ME   Media 3.2—Finding and Adding Web Email Contacts
Access this video file through your registered Web Edition at
my.safaribooksonline.com/9780132117029/media.

 LET ME TRY IT

Find and Add Web Email Contacts on Facebook

To find and add your web email contacts, follow these steps:

1. In the upper-right corner of the Facebook page, click the Find Friends link.
   Alternatively, click the Friends link on the left menu of the Home page and
   then click Find Friends in the list of menu options that appears.

2. On the Friends page, click the Find Friends link to the right of the email
   service you want to search, such as Windows Live Hotmail, Yahoo!, AOL,
   Comcast, and so forth (see Figure 3.1). If your email service isn't listed
   (such as Gmail), click the Find Friends link to the right of the Other Email
   Service section.

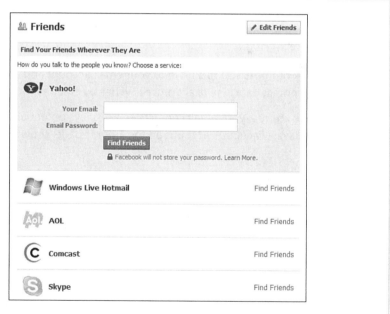

Figure 3.1   *You can search for your email contacts with numerous email services.*

Although Facebook works with most popular email services, it doesn't work with all services. If your system is incompatible, Facebook replaces the Password field with the message: **We can't import contacts from this address yet**. If this happens, you must create a contact file and import it, as described in "Connecting with Your Desktop Email Contacts on Facebook" later in this chapter.

3. Enter the requested information, which varies by email service. For example, Facebook could prompt you to enter a username, email address, password, and so forth (see Figure 3.2).

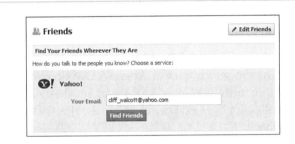

Figure 3.2   *Enter the required data so that Facebook can find and import your contacts.*

4. Click the Find Friends button.

5. Facebook prompts you to sign in to your email account and allow it access to your contact data. The exact process varies by email service.

6. Facebook imports your email contacts and displays potential matches who already have a Facebook account on the Friends page, shown in Figure 3.3.

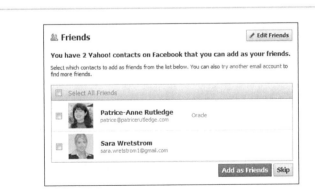

Figure 3.3   *View your matches on the Friends page.*

7. Select the checkbox next to the people you want to add as friends and then click the Add as Friends button. Facebook sends your requests automatically.

8. Next, Facebook prompts you to invite friends and family who aren't already Facebook users, shown in Figure 3.4. Select the checkbox next to the people you want to invite and click the Send Invites button. Facebook sends an email invitation to these people, prompting them to join Facebook and add you as a friend.

Figure 3.4   *Invite your friends who don't use Facebook yet.*

If you send someone a friend request by mistake and want to cancel it, you can do so on that person's Facebook profile (search by name in the search box at the top of the page). The Friend Request Sent box to the right of that person's name confirms that you sent a request. To cancel, click the Cancel Friend Request link under this person's photo.

Connecting with Coworkers on Facebook

When you signed up for an account, Facebook prompted you to enter information about your current and former employers. Facebook uses this data to search for potential coworkers.

 SHOW ME   Media 3.3—Finding and Adding Coworkers
Access this video file through your registered Web Edition at
my.safaribooksonline.com/9780132117029/media.

LET ME TRY IT

Find and Add Coworkers on Facebook

To find and add coworkers, follow these steps:

1. In the upper-right corner of the Facebook page, click the Find Friends link. Alternatively, click the Friends link on the left menu on the Home page and then click Find Friends in the list of menu options that appears.

2. On the Friends page, scroll down to the Other Tools sections and click the Find Friends link.

3. From the list of options (see Figure 3.5), click the Find Coworkers from [Employer Name] link that matches the employer you want to search. The exact names of the links on your screen vary based on the employer information you entered on Facebook.

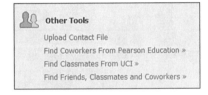

Figure 3.5   *Click the appropriate link to search for coworkers.*

4. Facebook opens the Find Friends from Different Parts of Your Life page, displaying a list of people from your workplace. To further narrow your results, select from the filters on the left side of the page.

If you haven't entered work information on your Facebook profile, clicking the Find Friends, Classmates, and Coworkers link also opens the Find Friends from Different Parts of Your Life page.

5. Click the Add as Friend link below the person you want to add as a friend. The Send [Person's Name] a Friend Request? dialog box opens, as shown in Figure 3.6.

6. Click the Add a Personal Message link to display a text box where you can write a message to the person you want to add as a friend. Adding a personal message is particularly important if you haven't seen this person in a while.

Figure 3.6 *Send your coworkers a friend request to connect on Facebook.*

Optionally, you can choose to receive text messages via SMS any time a friend posts a Facebook update or add someone to a friend list. These options don't appear if you haven't set up Facebook Mobile or created a friend list yet.

7. Click the Send Request button to send your friend request. Facebook sends your request and alerts this person that a new friend request is pending.

Alternatively, go to www.facebook.com/srch.php?coworker while logged in to Facebook to search for coworkers.

Connecting with Classmates on Facebook

When you signed up for an account, Facebook prompted you to enter information about the high school and universities you attended. Facebook uses this data to search for current and former classmates.

 LET ME TRY IT

Find and Add Classmates on Facebook

To find and add classmates, follow these steps:

1. In the upper-right corner of the Facebook page, click the Find Friends link. Alternatively, click the Friends link on the left menu and then click Find Friends in the list of menu options that appears.

2. On the Friends page, scroll down to the Other Tools sections and click the Find Friends link.

3. From the list of options, click the Find Classmates from [School Name] link that matches the school you want to search. The exact names of the links on your screen vary based on the educational information you entered on Facebook.

4. Facebook opens the Find Friends from Different Parts of Your Life page, displaying a list of potential classmates. To further narrow your results, select from the filters on the left side of the page.

If you haven't entered school information on your Facebook profile, clicking the Find Friends, Classmates, and Coworkers link also opens the Find Friends from Different Parts of Your Life page.

5. Click the Add as Friend link below the person you want to add as a friend. The Send [Person's Name] a Friend Request? dialog box opens (refer to Figure 3.6).

6. Click the Add a Personal Message link to display a text box where you can write a message to the person you want to add as a friend. Adding a personal message is particularly important if you haven't seen this person in a while.

Optionally, you can choose to receive text messages via SMS any time a friend posts a Facebook update or add someone to a friend list. These options don't appear if you haven't set up Facebook Mobile or created a friend list yet.

7. Click the Send Request button to send your friend request. Facebook sends your request and alerts this person that a new friend request is pending.

Alternatively, go to www.facebook.com/srch.php?classmate while logged in to Facebook to search for classmates.

Connecting with Your Desktop Email Contacts on Facebook

If you use a desktop email application such as Microsoft Outlook, Outlook Express, Apple Mail, or Mozilla Thunderbird, you can import a contact file that Facebook searches for potential matches. Depending on the email application you use, you can do this in one of two ways: have Facebook import your contacts directly or create a contact file and import it into Facebook.

A contact file is any file in a standardized format that contains information about friends and other people, typically called contacts. An example of a contact file type is friends.csv or contacts.ldif.

SHOW ME   Media 3.4—Uploading a Contact File
Access this video file through your registered Web Edition at
my.safaribooksonline.com/9780132117029/media.

LET ME TRY IT

Add Friends by Uploading a Contact File

To upload a contact file, follow these steps:

1. In the upper-right corner of the Facebook page, click the Find Friends link. Alternatively, click the Friends link on the left menu and then click Find Friends in the list of menu options that appears.

2. On the Friends page, scroll down to the Other Tools sections and click the Find Friends link.

3. From the list of options, click the Upload Contact File link to display additional fields (see Figure 3.7).

4. From here, you have two choices for importing contacts:

    • If you use Microsoft Outlook, Outlook Express, or Windows Contacts, click the Find My Windows Contacts button. If a security prompt appears, allow Facebook to access your data. Facebook searches for your contacts and imports them.

- If you use another email system such as Mozilla Thunderbird or Apple Mail, you can create a contact file for Facebook to upload. Click the Browse button to select your file and then click the Upload Contacts button. If you don't want Facebook to access your Outlook data directly, you can also use this method for importing Outlook contacts. Another option is to create a contact file for your LinkedIn contacts.

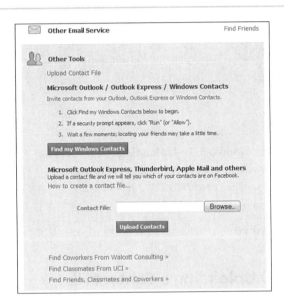

Figure 3.7   *Choose to have Facebook search for your desktop mail file or upload a contact file you created.*

If you're not sure how to create a contact file, click the How to Create a Contact File link to view step-by-step instructions for a variety of email systems.

5. Facebook imports your email contacts and displays potential matches who already have a Facebook account on the Friends page (refer to Figure 3.3).

6. Select the checkbox next to the people you want to add as friends and then click the Add as Friends button. Facebook sends your requests automatically.

7. Next, Facebook prompts you to invite friends and family who aren't already Facebook users (refer to Figure 3.4). Select the checkbox next to the people you want to invite and click the Send Invites button. Facebook sends an email invitation to these people, prompting them to join Facebook and add you as a friend.

If you use your desktop email system for something other than personal use, your business contacts might show up in the import list. Double-check this list. You might not want to send a Facebook invite to your boss, an outside organization, or a vendor.

Inviting Friends Who Aren't on Facebook Yet

You aren't limited to adding friends who already have a Facebook account. You can also invite friends who don't use Facebook yet, encouraging them to sign up and add you as a friend.

 **LET ME TRY IT**

Invite Your Friends to Join Facebook

To invite friends to join Facebook, follow these steps:

1. Select Edit Friends from the Account drop-down menu in the upper-right corner of any Facebook page.

2. On the left menu, click the Invite Friends link. Facebook opens the Invite Your Friends page.

3. Enter the email addresses of the friends you want to invite to join Facebook, separating each with a comma (see Figure 3.8).

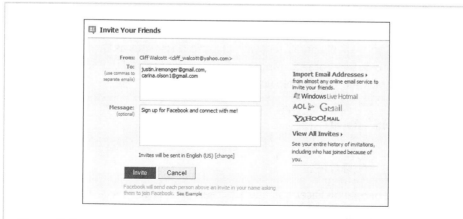

Figure 3.8   *Enter the email addresses of friends you want to invite to Facebook.*

4. Enter an optional message.

5. Click the Invite button. Facebook sends each person an email invitation to join the site and add you as a friend.

To view a history of your invites, click the View All Invites link to open the Review Your Invites and Imported Contacts page, shown in Figure 3.9.

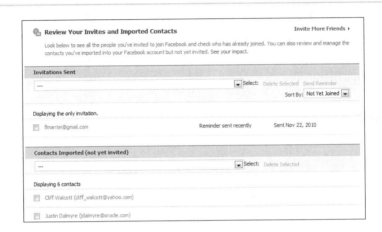

Figure 3.9   *Review the people you invited to Facebook and the contacts you imported.*

On this page, you can monitor your sent invitations as well as the contacts you imported. If you want to delete this data, click the following link: Click Here to Remove All Contacts on This Page and All Contacts from Your Phonebook.

Searching for People on Facebook

After adding your email contacts, coworkers, and classmates as Facebook friends, you might decide there are still more people you want to add to your Facebook network. A quick search can help you find them.

 **LET ME TRY IT**

Search for People

To search for people on Facebook and add them as friends, follow these steps:

1. Type your search term in the quick search box that appears at the top of every Facebook page. If you're searching for a person you know, this is usually the person's name.

You can also search for people you don't know using keywords such as an employer, school, or other words that are associated with the type of people you want to find. For example, you could enter "sommelier" to find wine experts or "soccer" to find people who share your love of that sport.

2. As you type, Facebook displays potential search results (see Figure 3.10). These search results can include Facebook profiles, pages, groups, and more. For example, when you search for my name (Patrice-Anne Rutledge), Facebook lists both my personal profile and my business page.

Figure 3.10   *Facebook makes it easy to search for people.*

3. If Facebook finds the right person, click that person's name to open the associated profile. Here, you can click the Add as Friend button to add this person as a friend. Remember to include a personal message if you don't know this person well, explaining why you want to connect on Facebook.

4. If the person you're looking for doesn't appear in the top six results, or you want to view more people, click the See More Results for [Person's Name] link.

5. On the All Results page, Facebook lists everything that matches your keywords, including people, pages, groups, and more.

6. To narrow your search results, click one of the links on the left menu, shown in Figure 3.11. These include People, Pages, Groups, Applications, Events, Web Results, Posts by Friends, or Posts by Everyone. For example, click the People link to display only individual Facebook profiles.

Figure 3.11   *Narrow your search results to make it easier to find the right person.*

When you narrow your search results to display only people, Facebook enables you to filter your results even further—by location, education, or workplace.

7. When you find the person you're looking for, click the Add as Friend button to open the Send [Person's Name] a Friend Request? dialog box.

You might not see the Add as Friend next to every listing in the search results. For example, the Like button appears next to Facebook pages. If you're already friends, no button appears.

8. Click the Add a Personal Message link to explain why you're sending a request.

9. Click the Send Request button. Facebook sends your request and alerts this person that a new friend request is pending.

Although it can be fun to search Facebook for potential friends and send them friend requests, don't overdo it. Facebook discourages its users from sending too many friend requests at once and can suspend your account if it feels that you're spamming fellow Facebook users. To be safe, limit your friend requests to people you don't know to about 20 per day and vary your personalized message. Note that this caution doesn't apply to adding friends who are your email contacts, coworkers, or classmates.

Viewing and Accepting Friend Requests

In addition to sending friend requests, you can also receive friend requests from other Facebook users who want to befriend you. The Friend Requests icon that appears in the top-left corner of every Facebook page lets you know how many pending friend requests you have whenever you log on to Facebook (see Figure 3.12).

Figure 3.12   *One person is waiting to become your friend on Facebook.*

 SHOW ME   Media 3.5—Viewing and Accepting Friend Requests
Access this video file through your registered Web Edition at
my.safaribooksonline.com/9780132117029/media.

Click this icon to display a drop-down menu of your most recent requests. If you recognize a name on this list, you can click the Confirm button to confirm the request. If you're not sure, click the Not Now button to temporarily hide the request. You can also click the name of the person sending the request to view the corresponding Facebook profile.

If one of your friends sent you friend suggestions, these people also display on this drop-down menu. The Add as Friend button and Ignore button appear to the right of a person who was suggested to you, but didn't personally send you a friend request.

To view all your requests, click the See All Friend Requests link. The Requests page lists all your pending friend requests as well as friend suggestions from your existing friends.

On this page, you can click the

- Name of a person to view the corresponding Facebook profile. This is particularly useful if you don't recognize the person who sent the friend request and you need to make a decision whether or not to accept.

- Confirm button to the right of any person you want to confirm as a friend. From here, you can optionally add this person to a friend list, write on his wall, chat with him, or suggest new friends to him.

- Not Now button to hide the request from view. Facebook doesn't add this person as a friend.

- Hide All Requests button to temporarily hide your requests from view.

- See [Number] Hidden Requests link to view requests you've hidden. The number corresponds to the number of hidden requests you have. This appears only if you have hidden requests.

- Delete Request button to the right of a person whose request you want to remove from your list. Facebook doesn't add this person as a friend.

- Delete All link to delete all pending requests.

Suggesting Friends

If you'd like to connect your Facebook friends with other likeminded people, you can suggest new friends for them. This is particularly useful for people who are new to Facebook. For example, let's say that your coworker Amy just signed up for Facebook and has only three friends right now. You and Amy have many friends in common in the real world (who also have Facebook accounts), so you decide to suggest that Amy add these people as Facebook friends.

 **LET ME TRY IT**

Suggest New Friends to Your Existing Friends

To suggest new friends for one of your existing Facebook friends, follow these steps:

1. Go to the Facebook profile of the friend for whom you want to suggest new friends. To find a specific friend, enter your friend's name in the search box at the top of the Facebook page.

2. Click the Suggest Friends button in the upper-right corner of your friend's profile. The Suggest Friends for [Person's Name] dialog box opens. This dialog box displays the name and photo of all your friends, listed in alphabetical order by first name.

If your friend has been using Facebook for a while, you might find the Suggest Friends link at the bottom of the left column on his Facebook profile.

3. Select the friends you want to suggest by clicking their names. Optionally, you can search for friends by typing their name in the Find Friends text box. If you have a large network of friends on Facebook, selecting a friend list or network from the Filter Friends drop-down list helps you find the most appropriate friends to suggest.

4. To verify the friends you are suggesting, click the Selected link to display the list.

5. Click the Send Suggestions button to send suggestions to your friend. The people you suggest appear in the drop-down list when you click the Friend Requests icon at the top of the Facebook page as well as on the Requests page.

Your friend can then choose to add these people as friends or ignore your suggestions.

Removing Friends

If you decide you no longer want to maintain one of your Facebook friendships, you can remove that person as a friend. To remove someone as a Facebook friend, go to that person's profile and click the Unfriend link at the bottom of the left column. Facebook removes that person as a friend—and removes access to your friends-only content—but doesn't notify your former friend that you did this.

Be sure to use this feature wisely. Don't remove people from your Facebook network just because you haven't seen them in a while. If someone is truly harassing you, however, you can report this behavior to Facebook by clicking the Report/Block This Person link below the Unfriend link.

4

Communicating with Your Friends

Facebook offers a variety of ways to communicate with your friends, including sharing content on your profile Wall and the News Feed, exchanging private messages, and chatting online. The Wall is the focal point of your Facebook communication, where you can share updates, photos, videos, and links with your friends and they can like, share, and comment on what you post.

In this chapter, you explore Facebook's many options for communicating with your friends. You can also watch videos that show you how to share your status, share a website link, tag post content, create a friend list, communicate with friends on your Wall, send messages, view and reply to a conversation, and use Facebook Chat.

Sharing Content with Your Friends

Sharing content with friends is one of the most popular activities on Facebook. You can share the following:

- **Status**—Create a quick text update that lets your Facebook friends know what's new in your life. See "Sharing Your Status" later in this chapter for more information.

- **Photo**—Upload photos from your computer, take a photo with a webcam and upload it, or create a photo album with multiple photos. See Chapter 7, "Publishing Photos," for more information.

- **Link**—Share a link to an interesting website, blog post, or article with your Facebook friends. See "Sharing a Website Link" later in this chapter for more information.

- **Video**—Upload a video from your computer or record a video with your webcam and upload it. See Chapter 8, "Publishing Videos," for more information.

If you don't want to share content publicly, consider sending a private message, covered in "Using Facebook Messages" later in this chapter. Another option is to create a group to communicate only with specific likeminded people who share your interests. For more information about Facebook groups, see Chapter 10, "Joining and Creating Groups."

The Share menu, located at the top of your home page or profile, enables you to post the content you want to share. Figure 4.1 shows an example of this menu.

Figure 4.1   *Use the Share menu to quickly share content with your Facebook friends.*

Content you share displays in two places, depending on the privacy settings you select:

- **Your Facebook Wall**—Your Wall (see Figure 4.2) is the centerpiece of your Facebook profile, displaying the content you share, your friends' likes and comments about this content, and other Facebook activities (such as when you have a new friend, like a page, and so forth). Facebook also allows your friends to post their own content on your Wall (see Chapter 6, "Safeguarding Your Information on Facebook," to learn how to disable this). Posting on your Wall is the most popular way to communicate with your Facebook friends.

- **The News Feed**—The News Feed displays on both your home page and your friends' home page, enabling your entire Facebook network to see what's new with you, even if they don't visit your profile directly (see Figure 4.3). See Chapter 5, "Keeping Up to Date with Your Friends," for more information about the News Feed.

Before you start sharing on Facebook, it's worthwhile to spend a few minutes thinking about exactly what information you should—and shouldn't—share. First, consider your audience. Who is in your Facebook network? Are they family members and personal friends? Or are you friends with clients, coworkers, or even your boss? Before you share anything, think about who could see what you post and what you feel comfortable sharing with them.

Figure 4.2   *Your Wall is the centerpiece of your Facebook profile.*

Figure 4.3   *Keep up with the latest news from your friends on the News Feed.*

Sharing Your Status

Sharing your status is the fastest and easiest way to let your Facebook friends know what's new in your life.

> You can also share your status from your mobile device. See Chapter 9, "Your Mobile Access to Facebook," for more information.

 SHOW ME   Media 4.1—Sharing Your Status
Access this video file through your registered Web Edition at
my.safaribooksonline.com/9780132117029/media.

 LET ME TRY IT

Share Your Status

To share your status on Facebook, follow these steps:

1. Click the Home or Profile link in the upper-right corner of any Facebook page.

2. Click the Status link in the Share menu below your News Feed or profile information (refer to Figure 4.1).

3. In the text box that displays (see Figure 4.4), type your status update. Optionally, you can tag people or pages in your status. See "Tagging Post Content" later in this chapter for more information.

4. By default, Facebook shares your status update with everyone. To restrict this, click the down arrow to the right of the lock icon and select one of the following options:

   - **Friends and Networks**—Share with your friends and fellow members of the Facebook networks you belong to.
   - **Friends of Friends**—Share with your friends and their friends.
   - **Friends Only**—Share only with your own friends.
   - **Customize**—Open the Custom Privacy dialog box where you can limit the viewing of this status to specific friends or people on a friend list. You can also prevent selected friends from viewing this content.

5. Click the Share button. Facebook publishes your content as a post on your Wall. This content also displays in your friends' News Feeds based on the privacy options you chose, if any.

Figure 4.4   *Share your status with your Facebook friends.*

Figure 4.5 shows a sample status posted on a Facebook Wall.

Figure 4.5   *A sample status on a Facebook Wall.*

Sharing a Website Link

If you find an interesting website, blog post, or news article, you can share it with your friends. This is also a good way to spread the word about your own web content, but be careful not to overdo this. You don't want to lose friends by focusing on self-promotion too much.

 SHOW ME   Media 4.2—Sharing a Website Link
Access this video file through your registered Web Edition at
my.safaribooksonline.com/9780132117029/media.

 LET ME TRY IT

Share a Website Link

To share a website link, follow these steps:

1. Click the Home or Profile link in the upper-right corner of any Facebook page.

2. Click the Link link in the Share menu below your News Feed or profile information (refer to Figure 4.1).

3. Type the link in the text box that begins with http://. If the link is long, copy and paste it to ensure accuracy.

4. Click the Attach button. Facebook searches for the link you attached and displays a title, thumbnail image, and summary of its content. Figure 4.6 shows a sample link.

Figure 4.6 *Share interesting web content with your friends.*

5. If you don't like the default thumbnail image, click the right arrow to scroll through your options. Alternatively, click the No Thumbnail checkbox to remove the thumbnail image.

6. If you want to edit the title or summary, click its text and make your changes.

7. By default, Facebook shares your link with everyone. To restrict this, click the down arrow to the right of the lock icon and select one of the following options:

   - **Friends and Networks**—Share with your friends and fellow members of the Facebook networks you belong to.
   - **Friends of Friends**—Share with your friends and their friends.
   - **Friends Only**—Share only with your direct friends.
   - **Customize**—Open the Custom Privacy dialog box where you can limit the viewing of this status to specific friends or people on a friend list. You can also prevent selected friends from viewing this content.

8. Optionally, add your own comments in the Say Something About This Link text box.

9. Click the Share button. Facebook publishes your content as a post on your Wall. This content also displays in your—and your friends'—News Feed.

Figure 4.7 shows a sample link posted on a Facebook Wall.

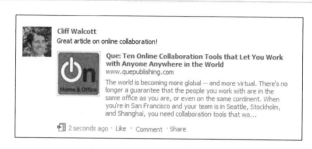

Figure 4.7   *A sample website link on a Facebook Wall.*

Tagging Post Content

When you post content on Facebook, you can make it more interactive by tagging the people, pages, groups, events, and applications related to that content. For example, if you just ate at a great restaurant with some friends, you could post a status update about it, tagging your friends and the restaurant (see Figure 4.8).

Figure 4.8   *Use tags to make your status updates more interactive.*

You can add tags in the following places:

- Status updates you post on your profile, your friends' profiles, or a page you like

- Text boxes that appear below a link, photo, or video you're sharing

Be aware that you can tag only friends, pages you like, groups you belong to, apps you use, and so forth rather than all content on Facebook.

SHOW ME   Media 4.3—Tagging Post Content
Access this video file through your registered Web Edition at
my.safaribooksonline.com/9780132117029/media.

LET ME TRY IT

Tag Friends, Pages, and Other Facebook Content

To tag your friends, pages, or other Facebook content in a post, follow these steps:

1. In a location that accepts tags, type the @ symbol in the text box and continue typing the name of the friend, page, group, event, or application you want to tag. As you type, Facebook displays a drop-down menu of potential matches, shown in Figure 4.9.

Figure 4.9   *Tag your friends or pages you like.*

2. Select the name you want to tag from the menu of options.

3. Continue steps 1 and 2 until you finish tagging. You can tag multiple items in a post, but be careful not to overdo this.

Facebook replaces the @ symbol and name with a link to the item you tagged. Anyone who sees your posts can click the item you tagged, if permitted by the existing privacy settings.

If you tag a friend, Facebook notifies the friend of the tag and of any comments on a post with that tag.

Creating and Using Friend Lists

A friend list enables you to organize your Facebook friends by category. For example, you could create friend lists for family members, coworkers, former classmates, members of a club or organization you belong to, and so forth.

Friend lists are useful for specifying who can view the content you share (see "Sharing Content with Your Friends" earlier in this chapter). You can also use friend lists to filter the content you view on your News Feed. See Chapter 5 for information.

To add a new friend to an existing list, click the Add to List button that displays after confirming your friendship.

 SHOW ME   Media 4.4—Creating a Friend List
Access this video file through your registered Web Edition at
my.safaribooksonline.com/9780132117029/media.

 LET ME TRY IT

Create a Friend List

To create a friend list, follow these steps:

1. Select Edit Friends from the Account drop-down menu in the upper-right corner of any Facebook page.

2. On the Friends page, click the Create a List button to open the Create New List dialog box, shown in Figure 4.10.

3. Enter a name for your list in the Enter a Name text box. For example, you could call your list Work Friends or Family.

4. To add a friend to your list, click this person's photo on the Create New List dialog box. Facebook adds the friend to the list and indicates this by placing a checkmark in the lower left corner of the photo (see Figure 4.11). The number to the right of the Selected link increases by one.

If you have many friends and it's hard to find them in the dialog box, type the name of a person you want to add in the Start Typing a Name text box. Facebook searches for this person and displays the results.

5. Continue adding friends until your list is complete.

6. Click the Create List button to close the Create New List dialog box and create your list.

Figure 4.10   *Create friend lists to protect your privacy and filter what you see on your News Feed.*

Figure 4.11   *Select specific friends for your friend list.*

Editing a Friend List

You can easily add or remove friends from a friend list.

LET ME TRY IT

Edit a Friend List

To edit a friend list, follow these steps:

1. Select Edit Friends from the Account drop-down menu in the upper-right corner of any Facebook page.

2. On the Friends page, click the link for the friend list you want to edit.

3. On the friend list page (see Figure 4.12 for an example), you can

   - Rename your list by clicking the Edit Name link to the right of the list name.

   - Add a new friend to the list by typing this person's name in the Type a Friend's Name to Add text box.

   - Add multiple new friends by clicking the Add Multiple button. The Edit List dialog box opens. This dialog box is nearly identical to the Create New List dialog box (refer to Figure 4.10). See the "Create a Friend List" section earlier in this chapter for more information about how to add friends using this dialog box.

   - Remove a friend by clicking the Remove from List (x) button to the right of this person's name.

   - Select or deselect a list name from the Edit Lists drop-down button that displays to the right of each person on this page.

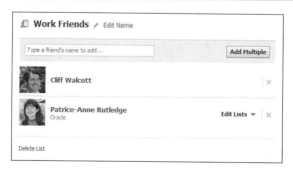

Figure 4.12 *View and modify your friend list.*

Deleting a Friend List

If you no longer need a friend list, you can delete it.

 LET ME TRY IT

Delete a Friend List

To delete a friend list, follow these steps:

1. Select Edit Friends from the Account drop-down menu in the upper-right corner of any Facebook page.

2. On the Friends page, click the link for the friend list you want to edit.

3. On the friend list page (refer to Figure 4.12), click the Delete List link.

4. In the Delete [List Name] dialog box, click the Confirm button to confirm deletion. Be aware that you can't restore a deleted friend list.

Communicating with Friends on Your Wall

One of the enjoyable aspects of posting content to your Wall is reading and responding to your friends' comments. After reading your post, your friends can

- Click the Like link to let you know they like your post.

- Click the Comment link to type a comment about your post. Comments appear below their associated post.

- Click the Share link to share your post on their wall. This option is available only for links, photos, and videos.

 SHOW ME   Media 4.5—Communicating with Friends on Your Wall
Access this video file through your registered Web Edition at
my.safaribooksonline.com/9780132117029/media.

Facebook notifies you that someone has liked or commented on your post through the Notifications icon in the upper-left corner of the Facebook page. In Figure 4.13, you can see that this Facebook user has two new notifications.

Click the Notifications icon to view a drop-down menu of your latest notifications (see Figure 4.14). You can click a specific notification to view it or click the See All Notifications link to view a list of your notifications.

Figure 4.13   *Click the Notifications icon to see what your friends have to say.*

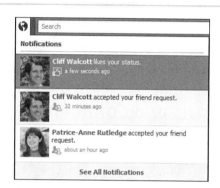

Figure 4.14   *View a list of the people who have liked or commented on your post.*

Responding to Wall Comments and Activity

In addition to viewing the comments your friends make about your Wall posts, you can add your own comments, either to respond to your friends' comments or to provide more information. You can also like a specific comment left by a friend.

 LET ME TRY IT

Add a Comment to Your Wall Post

To add a comment to one of your own wall posts, follow these steps:

1. Locate the post you want to add a comment to on your Facebook Wall. (Click the Profile link in the upper-right corner of the screen if your Wall isn't visible.)

2. Type your text in the Write a Comment box below the original post. If none of your friends has commented yet, click the Comment link to open this box.

3. Click the Comment button to post your comment, as shown in Figure 4.15.

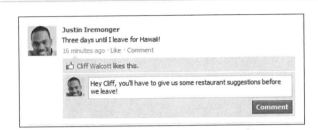

Figure 4.15 *Continue the conversation by adding your own comments to your Wall posts.*

Deleting Wall Posts and Comments

Although it's fun to post content on your Wall—and view your friends' commentary—there are times when you'll want to delete posts and comments on your Wall. For example, a friend could add a post or comment you don't want others to see or you could change your mind about something you posted.

 LET ME TRY IT

Delete Wall Posts and Comments

To delete Wall posts and comments, follow these steps:

1. Hover your mouse over the content you want to delete.

2. Click the Remove button (X) to the right of the post or comment.

3. Depending upon the type of content you're deleting and the person who posted it, one of the following happens (see Figure 4.16 for an example):

   • The Delete Post dialog box opens where you can click the Remove Post button to confirm deletion.

   • The Delete Comment dialog box opens where you can click the Delete button to confirm deletion.

   • A drop-down menu opens with options related to the post. For example, this menu could include any of the following options: Remove Post, Remove Post and Untag, Revoke Publishing Rights of [Application Name], Mark as Spam, Report as Abuse, and so forth.

4. Select the most appropriate option and confirm deletion.

Figure 4.16 *Facebook offers several options for deleting posts and comments.*

Using Facebook Messages

Facebook Messages offers much more than just a way to send private messages to your Facebook friends. With Facebook Messages, you can view traditional messages, text messages, and chat transcripts from a specific Facebook friend all in the same place. If you activate your optional Facebook email address, you can view email as well. Facebook refers to this comprehensive communication history as a conversation. You can have a conversation with one friend or a group conversation with multiple friends.

Facebook announced a major update to Messages in late 2010 and is rolling out this upgrade over time. If you haven't upgraded yet, go to http://www.facebook. com/about/messages and click the Request an Invitation button to request an upgrade to the new Facebook Messages.

Setting Up Facebook Messages

Because Facebook Messages integrates with your Facebook email account (@facebook.com), text messaging, and Facebook Chat, your first step is to set up the features you plan to use. All of these are optional. Depending on your previous experience with Facebook, they might already be active.

To view your setup options, click the Messages icon in the upper-left corner of the screen and click the See All Messages link in the drop-down menu.

At the top of the Messages page, the setup bar displays three links as shown in Figure 4.17.

If you don't see the setup bar on your page, scroll down to the bottom of the page where you can also access the setup links.

Figure 4.17   *Set up Facebook Messages to integrate email, text messaging, and chat.*

Your choices include the following:

- **Claim Your Facebook Email**—Activate your Facebook email address, which matches your public username. For example, if your username is annesmith then your email address would be annesmith@facebook.com. See "Activate Your Facebook Email Address" later in this chapter for more information.

- **Turn on Text Messaging**—Activate Facebook text messaging, which enables you to send and receive text messages as well as incorporate these messages into your Facebook conversations. See Chapter 9 for more information.

- **Go Online to Chat**—Activate Facebook Chat so that you can exchange instant messages with your friends real-time. Facebook also incorporates chat transcripts in your conversations. See "Using Facebook Chat" later in this chapter for more information.

 **LET ME TRY IT**

Activate Your Facebook Email Address

To activate your Facebook email address, follow these steps:

1. On the Messages page (refer to Figure 4.17), click the Claim Your Facebook Email link at the top of the page.

2. In the dialog box that opens, click the Activate Email button (see Figure 4.18).

3. Click the Next button to continue to set up Facebook text messaging. If you don't want to do so, click the Skip link.

After you activate your Facebook email address, people can use it to send you messages from any other email system such as Gmail, Hotmail, Yahoo! Mail, and so forth. Email messages from Facebook friends display on the Messages page. Messages from all other people display on your Other page.

You can also send messages to anyone with an email address with Facebook Messages.

Figure 4.18   *Facebook makes it easy to create your own email address.*

Sending Messages

There are several ways to send messages on Facebook. You can

- Go to the profile of the person to whom you want to send a message and click the Message button. Depending on your history with this person, one of the following occurs:

  - If you've never contacted this person before, the New Message dialog box opens.

  - If you have an existing conversation with this person, Facebook opens your conversation where you can add a new message to it. In this case, you are essentially replying to an existing conversation. See "Reply to an Existing Conversation" later in this chapter for more information.

  - If this person is online and is available for chat, the chat window opens instead. If you really want to send a message to a person who is online rather than chat, use the New Message dialog box to send the message instead.

- Click the Messages icon in the upper-left corner of the screen and then click the Send a New Message link to open the New Message dialog box.

- Click the New Message button on the Messages page to open the New Message dialog box.

You can also send messages to more than one person at a time. Facebook calls this a group conversation. See "Participating in Group Conversations" later in this chapter for more information.

In addition to sending people a message, you can also poke them, using the Poke button to the right of the Message button on their profile. A *poke* is an electronic nudge, just to let someone know that you're there. Facebook notifies the person you poke using the Notification icon. Compared to the other communication channels Facebook offers, pokes aren't particularly useful. In fact, pokes tend to annoy many people, so you should use them with caution.

SHOW ME   Media 4.6—Sending Messages
Access this video file through your registered Web Edition at
my.safaribooksonline.com/9780132117029/media.

LET ME TRY IT

Send a Message to Someone for the First Time

To send a message to someone on Facebook for the first time, follow these steps:

1. Go to the profile of the person to whom you want to send a message.

2. Click the Message button in the top-right corner of the page to open the New Message dialog box, shown in Figure 4.19.

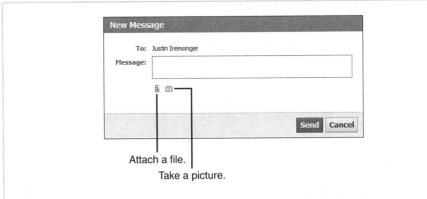

Figure 4.19   *Sending a message to someone on Facebook for the first time.*

3. Type your message in the text box. Be aware that Facebook messages don't use subject lines.

4. Optionally, you can

    •   Attach a file to your message by clicking the Attach a File button. The Choose File to Upload dialog box opens, where you can select a file from your computer. Click the Open button to attach the file.

    •   Take a picture or video with your webcam and attach to your message by clicking the Take a Picture or Video button. See Chapter 7 and Chapter 8 for more information.

5. Click the Send button to send your message. Facebook starts a new conversation with this person.

Viewing Facebook Messages

When you receive new messages, Facebook notifies you by placing a red square with the number of messages you have on the Messages icon, referred to as a red alert notification. See Chapter 5 for more information about red alert notifications.

Click the Messages icon to view a drop-down menu of the people who have most recently sent you messages (see Figure 4.20).

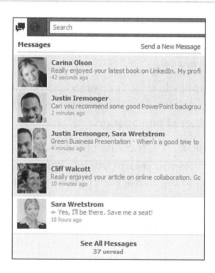

Figure 4.20   *Facebook lets you know when you have new messages.*

You can click the name of a person to open your conversation or click the See All Messages link to open the Messages page, shown in Figure 4.21.

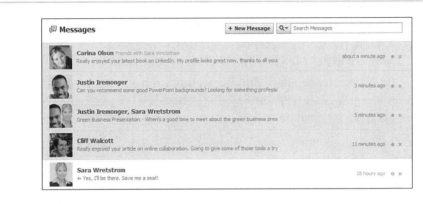

Figure 4.21 *Facebook displays messages from your friends.*

The Messages page includes only communication from your Facebook friends and not from pages, groups, and other applications you use. (They're available elsewhere.) It also doesn't include subject lines or individual messages. Instead, all your communication with a specific Facebook friend is grouped into one conversation with that person. For example, if your cousin Samantha has sent you five messages since you became Facebook friends, the Messages page displays one entry for Samantha, not five.

On the Messages page, you can

- Click the Messages link in the left column to display messages from your friends. This is the default view. The number to the right of the Messages link indicates the number of unread messages you have.

- Click the Other link in the left column to display other messages, such as messages from pages you like, groups you belong to, and people who aren't your friends. The number to the right of the Other link indicates the number of unread other messages you have.

- Click the New Message button to open the New Message dialog box where you can type a message to one or more friends. See "Sending Messages" earlier in this chapter for more information.

- Search for a message by name or keyword. See "Searching for Messages" later in this chapter for more information.

- Click the Archive (x) button to the right of a message to move it to your archived folder. To review archived messages, scroll down to the bottom of the page and click the Archived link. Archiving removes a message from the Messages page but doesn't delete it.

- Click the Mark as Read/Mark as Unread button (a small circle) to the right of a message to mark the message as read or unread. This button functions as a toggle you can turn on and off. Unread messages are highlighted in light blue; read messages have no highlight.

By default, anyone on Facebook can send you a message, even people who aren't your friends. See Chapter 6 for more information about limiting the people who can send you messages.

Viewing a Conversation

To view a conversation with a specific person, click the name of the sender on the Messages page or in the drop-down menu that opens when you click the Messages icon.

 SHOW ME   Media 4.7—Viewing and Replying to a Conversation
Access this video file through your registered Web Edition at
my.safaribooksonline.com/9780132117029/media.

If this is your first communication with someone, you view an individual message (see Figure 4.22).

Figure 4.22   *The first message from someone on Facebook.*

If you have already communicated with this person, Facebook displays your complete communication history. The most recent message in a conversation displays at the bottom. Figure 4.23 shows an example of a conversation.

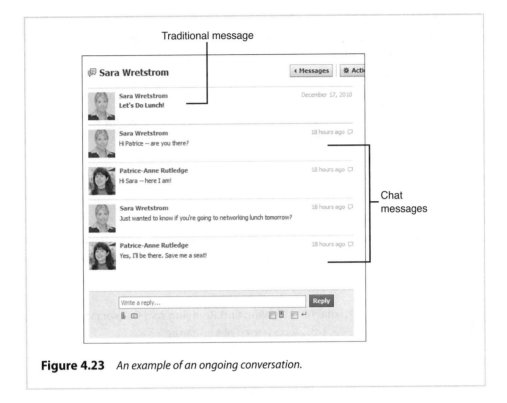

Figure 4.23   *An example of an ongoing conversation.*

Remember that your conversation with someone on Facebook includes messages, chats, texts, and emails (using your @facebook.com address), creating an ongoing record of all communication with this person.

You can reply to a message in a conversation by adding a new message to that conversation.

The Actions drop-down menu offers several additional options. You can select any of the following:

- **Mark as Unread**—Mark the conversation as unread. Facebook highlights this conversation in light blue on the Messages page.

- **Forward**—Forward individual messages from this conversation to another Facebook friend.

- **Archive**—Move the conversation to your archived folder. To review archived conversations, scroll down to the bottom of the page and click the Archived link. Archiving removes a conversation from the Messages page, but doesn't delete it.

- **Delete Messages**—Delete all messages, or just selected messages, from this conversation.

- **Report as Spam**—Report this conversation as spam to Facebook.

- **Report/Block User**—Report the sender to Facebook and block this person from sending you additional messages.

> Reporting someone to Facebook can have serious consequences to the sender. Be sure to report people only for offensive or unethical behavior and not just because you don't want to hear from a friend anymore. To unfriend someone, go to that person's profile and click the Unfriend link at the bottom of the left column.

- **Move to Other**—Move the conversation to the Other folder, where you can find messages from pages, groups, applications, and people who aren't your friends.

 LET ME TRY IT

Reply to an Existing Conversation

To reply to an existing conversation and add a new message to it, follow these steps:

1. Click the Messages icon in the upper-left corner of the screen.

2. Select a person from the drop-down menu or click the See All Messages link to select a person from the Messages page.

3. Facebook opens your conversation with this person.

4. Type your message in the text box at the bottom of the page, as shown in Figure 4.24.

5. Optionally, you can

   - Attach a file to your message by clicking the Attach a File button. The Choose File to Upload dialog box opens, where you can select a file from your computer. Click the Open button to attach the file.

   - Take a picture or video with your webcam and attach to your message by clicking the Take a Picture or Video button. See Chapter 7 and Chapter 8 for more information.

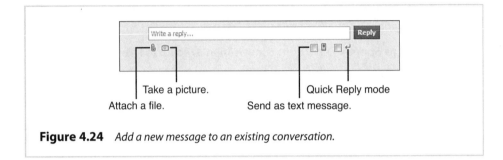

Figure 4.24 *Add a new message to an existing conversation.*

6. If you want to send your message as a text message as well, select the Also Send as a Text Message checkbox. Facebook notifies you if the message recipient hasn't activated text messaging yet and asks if you want to encourage this person to do so. See Chapter 9 for more information about text messages.

7. Click the Send button to send your message. Facebook adds it to the existing conversation.

If you want to speed up the sending process, you can select the Quick Reply Mode checkbox. Activating Quick Reply Mode enables you to send a message by pressing Enter on your keyboard rather than clicking the Send button. Be careful with this option, however. If you tend to write longer messages, you could accidentally send an incomplete message by pressing Enter when you really meant to start a new paragraph.

Searching for Messages

Even if you have a lot of Facebook messages, you can find a specific message easily by searching for it.

 LET ME TRY IT

Search for Facebook Messages

To search for a message on the Messages page, follow these steps:

1. In the Search text box, type the term you're searching for such as the name of a person or keyword.

2. From the drop-down menu that opens, shown in Figure 4.25, select the message you want to open.

Figure 4.25   *If you have a lot of messages, search for the one you want to view.*

3. If what you're searching for doesn't appear in the drop-down menu, you can

- Click the See More Results for [search term] link.
- Click the down arrow to the right of the Search button (small magnifying glass) to narrow your search to the following: unread messages, archived messages, sent messages, or email only.

Participating in Group Conversations

When you send a message to more than one person, you begin a group conversation. Group conversations are useful if you want to discuss a specific topic among a small group of Facebook friends. For example, let's say that you attended an event with your friends Trevor and Bianca and want to discuss this event with both of them. You can also maintain individual conversations with Trevor and Bianca as well.

Keep in mind that group conversations are most useful for short-term discussions with a small group of people. If you want to maintain an ongoing discussion with a larger group, consider creating a Facebook group instead. See Chapter 10 for more information.

 **LET ME TRY IT**

Start a Group Conversation

To start a group conversation, follow these steps:

1. Open the New Message dialog box by either:
    *   Clicking the Messages icon in the upper-left corner of the screen and then clicking the Send a New Message link.
    *   Clicking the New Message button on the Messages page.

2. In the New Message dialog box, start typing the name of the first person you want to include. As you type, Facebook displays a drop-down menu of matching friends. Select the name of the person you want.

3. Repeat Step 2 until you finish adding people (see Figure 4.26).

Figure 4.26   *Start a conversation with several people on Facebook.*

4. Type your message in the text box.

5. Optionally, you can
    *   Attach a file to your message by clicking the Attach a File button. The Choose File to Upload dialog box opens, where you can select a file from your computer. Click the Open button to attach the file.
    *   Take a picture or video with your webcam and attach to your message by clicking the Take a Picture or Video button. See Chapter 7 and Chapter 8 for more information.

6. If you want to send your message as a text message as well, select the Also Send as a Text Message checkbox. See Chapter 9 for more information about text messages.

7. Click the Send button to send your message. Facebook sends your message and starts a new group conversation.

Group conversations display on the Messages page just like a one-on-one conversation, with the names of all the people involved in the title. Click the list of names to open the conversation, as shown in Figure 4.27.

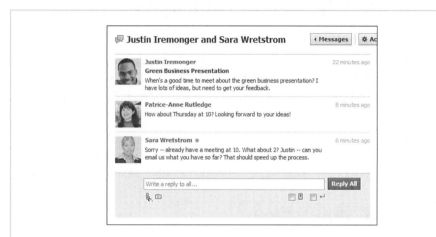

Figure 4.27   *Create group conversations with your Facebook friends.*

You can reply to a group conversation just as you would a regular conversation. The Action drop-down menu includes the same options as a regular conversation plus two other options:

- **Add People**—Open the Add People dialog box where you can add more people to the conversation.

- **Leave Conversation**—Open the Leave Conversation dialog box where you can confirm that you want to leave this conversation. Facebook notifies other people in the conversation that you've left and you won't receive any more messages from the conversation. You will still receive individual messages from people who are part of this conversation, however.

Using Facebook Chat

Facebook Chat offers yet another way to communicate on Facebook. Chat enables you to exchange real-time instant messages with another friend who is also online. Using Chat is a great option when you're looking for an immediate response to a question or post. Unlike Facebook's Wall, it is private between your friend and you.

SHOW ME   Media 4.8—Using Facebook Chat
Access this video file through your registered Web Edition at
my.safaribooksonline.com/9780132117029/media.

Understanding Facebook Chat Requirements

Facebook requires one of the following to use Chat:

- **A supported browser**—Supported browsers include Internet Explorer, Firefox, Google Chrome, or Safari. If you have browser issues, verify that you have the latest version and clear your browser's cache and cookies. Each browser requires different steps to clear this, so consult your browser's help file if you're not sure how to do this.

- **A desktop chat client**—Go to www.facebook.com/sitetour/chat.php to learn more about using a desktop chat client such as iChat, Adium, AIM, or Pigdin.

Exploring Facebook Chat

The Facebook Chat window displays in the lower-right corner of the screen, as shown in Figure 4.28. The number in this window lets you know how many of your Facebook friends are currently online.

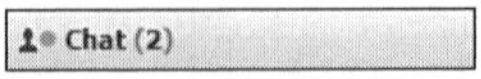

👤● Chat (2)

Figure 4.28   *Click to expand the Chat window and start chatting with your friends.*

Click the Chat window to expand it, displaying chat options and a list of friends potentially available to chat. Figure 4.29 shows a sample expanded Chat window.

You can close this expanded window by clicking the blue Chat box at the top of the window. Facebook Chat sorts friends first by friend lists, then by their online status, and then alphabetically by first name.

By default, Facebook displays the friends in all friend lists in this window, but you can specify which lists you want to display by clicking the Friend List button at the top of the window. You can also create a new friend list from this window. See "Creating and Using Friend Lists" earlier in this chapter for more information.

Figure 4.29 *See who is available for a quick chat on Facebook.*

You can go offline to a subset of your friends by placing those friends in a friend list, hovering over the icon to the right of the list, and clicking Go Offline.

Each friend's status displays as an icon to the right of their name in the Chat window. These are

- **Online**—These friends are active and available to chat. A green dot displays to the right of friends who are online.

- **Idle**—These friends are online, but haven't accessed Facebook within the last ten minutes. A half moon icon displays to the right of friends who are idle.

Anyone who isn't listed in the Chat window is either offline or has turned off chat functionality while on Facebook.

Chatting with a Friend

Facebook Chat allows you to chat with only one friend in the same Chat window, although you can have more than one Chat window open at the same time. You must be confirmed friends to chat with someone on Facebook.

If you want to chat with a group of people, check out the chat functionality of Facebook Groups, described in Chapter 10.

 LET ME TRY IT

Chat with a Friend

To chat with a friend, follow these steps:

1. Click the Chat window in the lower-right corner of the screen to expand it (refer to Figure 4.28).

2. Click the name of the person you want to chat with. Keep in mind that someone who is active (represented with a green dot) is more likely to respond than someone who is idle (represented with a half moon icon).

3. Type your chat message in the text box at the bottom of the Chat window. You can use regular text or emoticons such as :-) to represent a smile. See "Using Emoticons in Chat" for more information.

4. Press Enter to display your message at the top of the Chat window, as shown in Figure 4.30.

Figure 4.30   *Start chatting with a friend in the Chat window.*

5. Your friend's response, if any, displays in the Chat window below your message. You can continue typing and exchanging messages in the Chat window until you're done chatting.

6. Click the Close (x) button in the lower-right corner of the Chat window when you're finished chatting.

Facebook adds the messages from this chat to your Facebook Messages conversation with this friend (see Figure 4.31).

Figure 4.31 *View chat messages as part of your overall conversation with a friend.*

Specifying Facebook Chat Options

Facebook enables you to specify chat options by clicking the Options button at the top of the Chat window. Figure 4.32 shows a list of these options, which include the following:

- **Go Offline**—Remain on Facebook, but don't appear available to chat with friends. The offline chat status allows you to quickly check Facebook without being rude when you have limited time or are in a public place where you don't have privacy for a chat.

- **Re-order Lists**—Drag and drop your friend lists to re-order them.

- **Pop-out Chat**—Display your chat session in full screen.

- **Play Sound for New Messages**—Notify you of new messages with a sound. This is useful if you keep Facebook open while working with other applications.

- **Keep Online Friends Window Open**—Display your list of online friends.

- **Show Only Names in Online Friends**—Hide the image to the left of each friend's name.

Figure 4.32 *Control your chat experience in Facebook.*

Using Emoticons in Chat

Although Facebook Chat makes it easy to stay in touch with your friends, an online chat lacks nonverbal aspects of communication such as facial expressions or tone of voice. Fortunately, you can use emoticons to express what your Facebook friends can't see or hear. An emoticon offers a way to convey a facial expression through keyboard characters. For example, one of the most universally recognized emoticons is :-) to represent a smile.

Table 4.1 lists a selection of emoticons you can use in Facebook Chat:

Table 4.1　Facebook Chat Emoticons

Emoticon	Description
:)	Smile/happy
:(	Frown/sad
:/	Unsure
>:(	Grumpy
:'(	Cry
:*	Kiss
<3	Heart
;-)	Wink
:-D	Grin
8-|	Sunglasses
:-0	Gasp

Figure 4.33 shows an example of an emoticon in a chat conversation.

Figure 4.33   *Give your chat some personality with emoticons.*

This chapter helps you keep up with everything your friends post—without information overload.

5

Keeping Up to Date with Your Friends

One of the most enjoyable aspects of using Facebook is keeping up to date with friends. If you have a lot of friends or your friends post frequently, however, this enjoyable activity can soon become overwhelming. Fortunately, Facebook provides many different tools to pare down information and separate it into manageable amounts.

In this chapter, you learn how to keep up with your friends' Facebook activity. You can also listen to tips on how to manage this information without overwhelming yourself and watch videos that show you how to navigate your home page and News Feed, specify News Feed settings, view red alert notifications, and manage your email notifications.

Exploring Your Home Page

When you log in to Facebook, your initial view is that of your home page. Figure 5.1 shows a sample home page, filled with links to common Facebook tasks and the latest news from your friends.

TELL ME MORE Media 5.1—Keeping Up to Date with Your Facebook Friends

Access this audio recording through your registered Web Edition at my.safaribooksonline.com/9780132117029/media.

SHOW ME Media 5.2—Exploring Your Home Page

Access this video file through your registered Web Edition at my.safaribooksonline.com/9780132117029/media.

Figure 5.1   *Your home page shows you top news and provides links to Facebook's most popular features.*

The large center column of your home page displays your News Feed, which displays a continuously updated list of latest news from your friends and the pages you like. See "Exploring Your News Feed" later in this chapter for more information about your News Feed.

The left column of your home page lists four views that filter its content. These are

- **News Feed**—Displays your News Feed. This is the default home page view.

- **Messages**—Displays your message inbox. See Chapter 4, "Communicating with Your Friends," for more information about viewing and sending messages.

- **Events**—Displays and creates events. See Chapter 11, "Joining and Creating Events," for more information.

- **Friends**—Displays the Friends page where you can view your Facebook friends, send and respond to friend requests, and manage friend lists. See Chapters 3 and 4 for more information about adding and managing friends.

Below these views, Facebook provides links to your groups, applications, games, links, notes, and more. Some of these links include a counter number to their right. For example, the number 736 next to the Messages link means that you have 736 unread messages in your inbox.

The right column of your home page displays content that's personalized based on how you use Facebook. For example, you could see content related to upcoming events, sponsored content, questions, requests, and links to help you connect to more friends.

Exploring Your News Feed

Your Facebook News Feed (refer to Figure 5.1) appears in the center of your home page, where you can view the latest posts from your friends and the pages you like, photo tags, friend requests, event RSVPs, and even your own posts. Facebook continuously updates this feed with new content.

 SHOW ME   Media 5.3—Exploring Your News Feed
Access this video file through your registered Web Edition at
my.safaribooksonline.com/9780132117029/media.

From your News Feed, you can

- Click a link to view content in more detail, such as the name of a person, page, or post.

- Hover over a specific post and click the Remove (x) button to its right. A drop-down menu opens with options related to the post content. For example, you can hide the post; hide all posts from a specific person, page, or application; unlike the related page; or mark the post as spam.

- Click the Like, Comment, or Share link to interact with an individual post.

- Click the Older Posts link at the bottom of the page to view older news items.

- Click the Edit Options link at the bottom of the page. The Edit Your News Feed Settings dialog box opens, as shown in Figure 5.2, where you can specify the exact content you want to see in your News Feed, such as posts from the friends and pages you interact with most or all your friends and pages. You can also view a list of friends, pages, and apps you've hidden, and optionally unhide them by clicking the Remove (x) button to the right of their name.

If you're like the average Facebook user, you have about 130 Facebook friends. Depending on how active they are, this could amount to several hundred daily items in your News Feed. If you have more friends, or like numerous pages, your News Feed activity could increase exponentially. Fortunately, Facebook recognizes this dilemma and offers many ways to streamline what you see in your News Feed.

Figure 5.2 *Specify the exact content you want to see in your News Feed.*

By default, Facebook displays News Feed content using the Top News filter. Facebook uses a proprietary algorithm to determine what content appears as "top news," focusing on the number of people who comment on or like a certain post, the person who posted the content, and the type of content, such as a status update, photo, or video.

To display posts from your friends in real-time—essentially ignoring what Facebook considers "top news"—click the Most Recent link at the top of the News Feed (see Figure 5.3).

To filter your content even further, click the down arrow to the right of the Most Recent link. From this menu, you can choose the exact content to display: status updates, photos, links, or pages. You can also display content just from the friends you added to a specific friend list.

By default, this filter shows posts from your friends whom Facebook deems most relevant based on your past interactions.

To return to the default filter, click the Top News link.

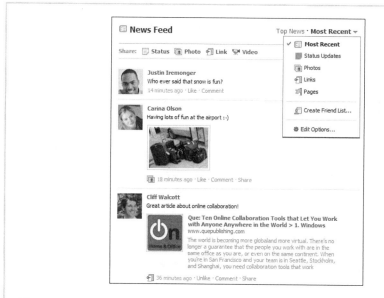

Figure 5.3 *Facebook displays your friends' activities in a continually updated News Feed.*

Viewing Friendship Pages

If you just want to view your interaction with one person on Facebook, a friendship page is the answer. Friendship pages let you view all the content you share with that person, which helps trace your common history on Facebook.

 **LET ME TRY IT**

View Friendship Pages

To view a friendship page for you and one of your Facebook friends, follow these steps:

1. Go to the profile of the person whose friendship page you want to view (use the search box at the top of Facebook if necessary).

2. At the top of the right column on this person's profile, click the See Friendship link.

The See Friendship link also appears when one of your friend's posts something on your Wall.

3. View the friendship page between you and your friend (see Figure 5.4), which displays all your shared content with this person including Wall posts, mutual friends, mutual events, pages and content you both like, as well as photos you're both tagged in.

Figure 5.4   *View your shared history with a Facebook friend.*

Understanding Facebook Notifications

Facebook makes it easier to keep track of friends, pages, groups, and applications by notifying you of their activity. You can view on-screen red alert notifications, receive pop-up notifications of actions that happen while you're online, and email notifications of recent activity.

Viewing Red Alert Notifications

Facebook alerts you to recent activity with the red alert notification icons in the upper-left corner of the screen (see Figure 5.5).

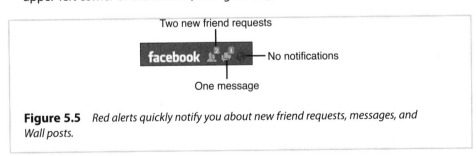

Figure 5.5   *Red alerts quickly notify you about new friend requests, messages, and Wall posts.*

SHOW ME   Media 5.4—Viewing Red Alert Notifications
Access this video file through your registered Web Edition at
my.safaribooksonline.com/9780132117029/media.

These icons are, from left to right:

- **Friend Requests**—View new friend requests and suggestions.

- **Messages**—View new messages in your inbox.

- **Notifications**—View Facebook activities such as Wall posts, friend comments or likes, event invitations, group invitations, and so forth.

When you receive a new message, friend request, or other notification, a red square with a number appears on the icon. In Figure 5.5, for example, you have two new friend requests, one new message, and no new notifications.

To view your red alert notifications, click one of the three icons to open a menu of your recent activity. To view older notifications, click the See All link at the bottom of the menu. Figure 5.6 shows an example of the Friend Requests menu.

Figure 5.6   *Quickly view your new friend requests.*

Viewing Pop-Up Notifications

Facebook displays real-time pop-up notifications when an action takes place while you're active on the site. For example, if a friend comments on one of your posts while you're on Facebook, a pop-up window displays in the bottom-right corner of the screen letting you know who just posted the comment. This notification appears for a few seconds and then disappears.

When Facebook notifies of you of an action via pop-up, it also notifies you with a red alert notification and an email notification (if you've activated this feature).

Managing Your Email Notifications

Facebook also offers email notifications for more than 60 types of actions that occur on the site. Although this is convenient, the volume of email can become overwhelming if you have lots of active Facebook friends. Fortunately, you can choose the exact notifications you want to receive and how you want to receive them.

SHOW ME   Media 5.5—Managing Your Email Notifications
Access this video file through your registered Web Edition at
my.safaribooksonline.com/9780132117029/media.

LET ME TRY IT

Specify the Email Notifications You Want to Receive

To control the email notifications Facebook sends you, follow these steps:

1. In the upper-right corner of the page, select Account Settings from the Account drop-down menu.

2. On the My Account page, select the Notifications tab, shown in Figure 5.7.

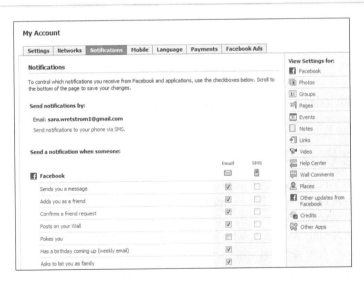

Figure 5.7   *Select the specific notifications you want to receive and how you want to receive them.*

3. In the Email column, select the checkbox for each notification you want to receive. The notifications fall into several categories. There are general Facebook notifications as well as notifications for actions related to photos, groups, pages, events, questions, notes, links, videos, Help Center

questions, Wall comments, places, other Facebook updates, credits, and applications.

> Some notifications are selected by default. Be sure to deselect the checkbox next to any default notification you don't want.

4. If you set up Facebook Mobile, the SMS column appears. Select the checkbox in this column for any SMS notifications you want to receive. SMS is available only for certain types of notifications. See Chapter 9, "Your Mobile Access to Facebook," for more information.

5. Click the Save Changes button to apply your notification settings.

Dealing with Fake Posts and Compromised Accounts

When is a friend's post, not posted by a friend? When your friend's Facebook account has been compromised. This happens more often than we would like to admit. Hackers or Facebook malcontents find ways to invite you to click on a link that compromises your account. It looks harmless, especially because it looks like it comes from a friend. If you are one of the unlucky ones, clicking the link sends you to an inappropriate site that changes the settings of your Internet browser and sends the bogus link to many of your Facebook friends via email and posts. A real-life hack is shown in Figure 5.8.

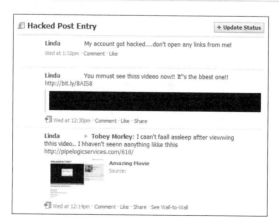

Figure 5.8   *An example of a bogus post.*

If you are extremely unlucky, clicking the link could install a mini application that tries to access your Facebook account without your knowing it and tries to gain access to your password. Here are some tips for detecting fake posts and links:

- Too many spelling errors in the title. We all make a few spelling errors when typing a post, but too many errors mean that it was purposely misspelled to bypass some virus detection system.

- If the title seems totally unbelievable, it normally is.

- Know your Facebook friends. Is the link or video typical of your friend? For example, if your 60-year-old uncle sends you a link to a skateboarding website he says is "wicked cool," it's probably not from him.

- Time is key. Look at the time the post was sent. Is your friend normally on at this time? If the post arrives while you are on Facebook, do the times match up within a few minutes? If not, don't open!

- Strange comments and behavior from your friends that make it seem like you should know what they are talking about. An example would be a post from a friend you haven't seen in a while who encourages you to click a link related to "that great party we both attended last night."

How to Clean a Hacked Account

So, you made a mistake and clicked when you should have deleted. Here are some quick steps to secure your computer and Facebook:

1. Close out all instances of your Internet browser immediately. Don't go back into Facebook until your computer is completely checked and clean.

2. Shut down and reboot your computer to remove any memory-only viruses. If you have issues booting up, you might need to go to another computer and download a boot up disk for virus scanning and repair.

3. Run a full virus scan of your computer. Some antivirus vendors allow you to scan your computer online for free.

4. After you verify the previous steps and your computer is clean, change your password.

LET ME TRY IT

Change Your Facebook Password

To change your Facebook password after your account has been compromised, follow these steps:

1. After your computer is cleaned, navigate to the Facebook login page (www.facebook.com).

2. Click the Forgot Your Password? link below the login and password boxes.

3. On the Identify Your Account page (see Figure 5.9), choose one of the three identification methods and enter the required information. You can identify your account by your email or phone number, your Facebook username, or your name and the name of one of your Facebook friends.

Figure 5.9 *Facebook requires you to identify your account before resetting your password.*

4. Click the Search button.

5. In the Security Check dialog box, type the required text and click the Submit button.

6. Click the Reset Password button to confirm that you want Facebook to reset.

7. Click the link in the email that Facebook sends you.

8. On the Enter a New Password page, enter and confirm your new password.

9. Click the Change Password button.

If you continually have your account hacked and nothing seems to be working correctly, you have two options. The first is to contact Facebook. Let Facebook know the state of your account, and indicate how to get in touch with you to see if they can resolve the issue. This step is important because Facebook has successfully won suits against hackers in the past. The second, and the most drastic, is to deactivate your account and start with a fresh account.

This chapter describes the common privacy threats and how to change privacy settings to safeguard your information on Facebook.

6

Safeguarding Your Information on Facebook

Understanding Facebook Privacy

To create and maintain social connections on Facebook, you have to share information and content. But it's important to know how to do so for the best Facebook experience while minimizing threats to your private information. The consequences from inadequately protecting your online information range from annoyance from spam and online embarrassment to identity theft or worse.

This chapter goes through securing your information given today's privacy threats.

 TELL ME MORE   Media 6.1—Facebook Privacy Threats Today and Commonsense Guidelines to Address Them
Access this audio recording through your registered Web Edition at
my.safaribooksonline.com/9780132117029/media.

Facebook Privacy Threats Today

They say that knowledge is power and Facebook has a plethora of information about you, your friends, and all of your interests. Think for a moment about the information that you have provided Facebook: birthday, work, education, friends, photos and videos of yourself and family, where you checked into using Places, maybe even your address and phone number. Now think about if this information was in the hands of someone who was not so friendly in nature, a hacker for example. Right about now you may be thinking about what information is on Facebook, who can access it, and most importantly, how to control what you share on Facebook and other connected sites. With this in mind, consider these real-life examples and the potential consequences:

- You leave the "keep me logged in" box checked on a public computer at the library and someone gains access to your account by logging in as you.

- Your coworker calls in sick but checks in using Facebook Places at a restaurant during her absence.

- A friend tags you in a picture from last night with your girlfriend. Your other girlfriend is not happy.

- You post a complaint about your boss, totally forgetting that your boss is a Facebook friend.

- You accept a friend request from a plastic frog, named "Freddi Staur" granting access to your email address, full birthday, workplace, current home address, and family photos. Freddi's profile was created by a security company and his name an anagram for "ID Fraudster."

- A Facebook member who isn't your Facebook friend convinces a friend in your network to look you up and pass along your profile information.

- An ex spies on your relationship status and photo albums using a "Fakebook" or profile with fake information.

- Someone copies personal information from your profile using Google without needing a Facebook account.

- Due to a bug, a Facebook game publically exposes the private chats between you and your friends and your personal information.

The moral is, be aware of common privacy threats and know how to protect your information.

Worried about a hacker finding another loophole in Facebook to exploit your profile or account? Though it does happen, Facebook also has a good track record of plugging these holes fast—sometimes the next day. But be aware that your information is valuable to some people, and mistakes do happen that compromise its protection.

Commonsense Guidelines

We walk through Facebook's privacy settings to safeguard your information, but first we cover up-front planning:

- **Don't post it**—Yes, abstinence works well. If you don't give Facebook touchy or personal information about yourself, it can't come back to haunt you regardless of Facebook settings or bugs.

- **Don't get carried away**—Remember why you joined Facebook? Keep your posted information relevant to that purpose. If you joined to find a job, it's best to include your professional accomplishments but not the wild photos from your last company's holiday party.

> When in doubt, do the "show and tell" check. If you'd be embarrassed showing or telling your parents or boss in real life, then leave it out of Facebook.

Manage Access to Your Account

Just as you don't leave your keys in your home door lock after you've left, you should probably not turn on Facebook's automatic login unless you absolutely trust those who can access that computer.

To turn off automatic login, uncheck the Keep Me Logged In box (see Figure 6.1). This prevents accidental or deliberate attempts to log in as you. The risk of account identify theft is greater if you use a shared computer at a library, a job, or at a school.

Figure 6.1   *Uncheck Keep Me Logged In to prevent unwanted access to your account.*

Because Facebook doesn't have an automatic log out, be sure to get in the habit of logging out. This quick step can easily prevent unwanted access to your account. To refresh your memory, you log out by going to the menu in the upper right, selecting Account, then Logout.

Changing Your Privacy Settings

Now that we've covered today's common threats and basic up-front approaches, we can adjust Facebook's privacy settings. These settings control the people, applications, and websites that can see your information. You can go with Facebook's defaults, their offered presets, or choose your own settings. Your final settings are designed to apply to all of Facebook's future offerings.

Although Facebook has changed its privacy controls several times, as a rule of thumb, assume the default settings are set at the most open level, meaning viewable by anyone on the Internet. This includes your name, status updates, and photos.

To access privacy settings, log in to Facebook, select Account from the upper right menu, and then Privacy Settings (see Figure 6.2).

Figure 6.2   *Select Account, then Privacy Settings to access Facebook's main privacy settings page.*

You then see Facebook's main privacy page. This is the master page to control all content you share on Facebook (see Figure 6.3).

Here's a breakout of the privacy page:

1. **Connecting on Facebook**—This controls who can see your basic directory information. This list includes your education and work history, current city, and visibility in Facebook's search engine. By default, all categories are viewable by everyone on the Internet and have options to limit the viewing audience.

2. **Sharing on Facebook**—This controls content you share (posts, photos), content others share about you (their comments on posts, tagging you in a photo), and contact information. Facebook uses the following presets:
   - **Everyone**—Viewable by everyone on the Internet without a Facebook account. This is for content that you want to share with a larger audience.
   - **Friends of Friends**—Viewable by friends of your friends. Use this for content relevant to this audience such as photos and videos.

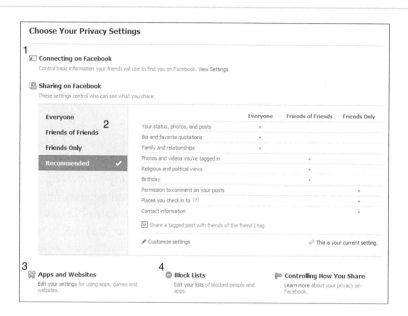

Figure 6.3   *Privacy Settings page.*

- **Friends Only**—Seen by Facebook friends only. Use this setting for contact information or other similar items meant for people you interact with directly.

- **Recommended**—Distributes across the previous three choices.

- **Customize**—After choosing one of four presets, you can customize your settings further. For example, you can control who can see the videos and photos you're tagged in that appear in your profile.

3. **Apps and Websites**—This controls what information applications and websites can access. This also controls your listing in public search engines such as Google and Instant Personalization (sites personalized using your public Facebook information).

4. **Block Lists**—This blocks specific people from contacting you or interacting with your information. This includes their event and application invites. Note that a blocked person might be able to still interact with you through applications and games you both use.

If you're pressed for time, consider adjusting your privacy settings for Contact Information (if you entered any), Profile Information, and Public Search Engines. These are controlled by # 1, 2, and 3 in Figure 6.3.

Control Basic Directory Information Sharing and Facebook Search Visibility

 SHOW ME   Media 6.2—Control Basic Directory Information Sharing and Facebook Search Visibility

Access this video file through your registered Web Edition at
my.safaribooksonline.com/9780132117029/media.

The Connecting on Facebook settings control the visibility of how you are found on Facebook and for parts of your profile used to find something in common with others. I've called this section basic directory information because these settings really control the directory content and tools others use to find you on Facebook. Because Facebook Search relies on basic directory information, it's included here. If you want to hide from public search engines, see the section with the same title, "Hide from Public Search Engines."

Depending on why you joined Facebook, you might be okay with accepting Facebook's default to make this content visible on the Internet and Facebook. After all, most of the Facebook experience is social, in which you connect with others. However, you still might want to hide parts of your profile. Perhaps you are using Facebook for fun and want to limit what your work colleagues see.

To control visibility using Facebook's groups, navigate to your Privacy Settings page (refer to Figure 6.9) and select View Settings under the Connecting on Facebook heading (refer to Figure 6.3, #1). Select the drop-down menu next to the setting you want to change and choose from the menu (see Figure 6.4).

The menu choices, except Customize, are described in the previous section, titled "Changing Your Privacy Settings," and are commonly used throughout Facebook. The menu choice of Customize is explained in the next section.

If you want to see how your profile looks after making changes, select Preview My Profile in the upper right, then type in a friend's name to see how your profile appears to him or her (see Figure 6.5). Select Back to Privacy Settings to return to the main privacy settings page.

Your name, gender, profile photo (should you choose to post one), and networks (should you choose to join one) are required to be visible to everyone and have no privacy control. Facebook does this so friends can find and recognize it's really you. You can limit the visibility of all other information.

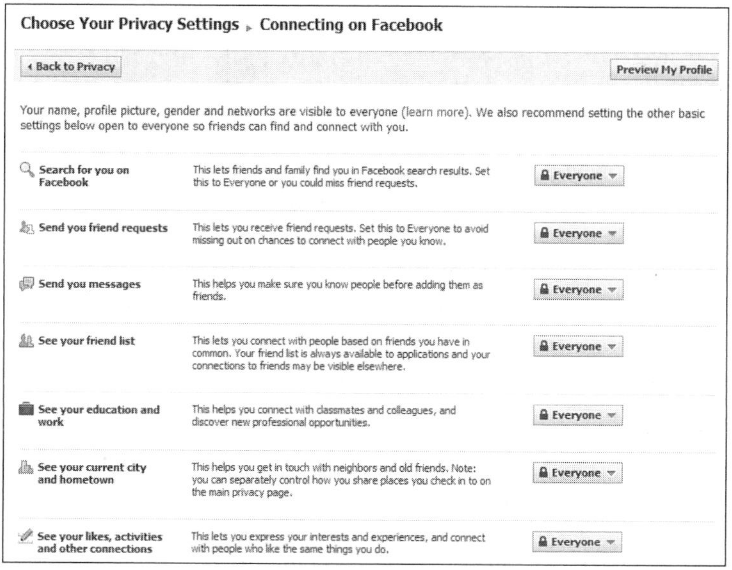

Figure 6.4   *Change privacy settings on the Connecting on Facebook page.*

Figure 6.5   *Type in a friend's name to see how your profile appears after changing privacy settings.*

Control Day-to-Day Content Sharing

SHOW ME   Media 6.3—Control Day-to-Day Content Sharing
Access this video file through your registered Web Edition at
my.safaribooksonline.com/9780132117029/media.

The controls for Sharing on Facebook can be found in the middle of the Privacy Settings page (refer to Figure 6.3, #2). These control the visibility of things you share about yourself and things others share about you, such as tagging you in a photo or commenting on your wall.

A photo owner can still share that photo with people you're not friends with, so remove the tag from the video or photo to prevent this from happening. This is described in Chapter 7, "Publishing Photos" and Chapter 8, "Publishing Videos."

Depending on how you want to use Facebook, you might be okay with accepting Facebook's Recommended preset, which distributes visibility across Everyone, Friends of Friends, and Friends Only (refer to Figure 6.3, see checkmark under #2). These groups are described in the previous section, "Changing Your Privacy Settings," and are used throughout Facebook. However, if you want to change the visibility of these items, you can select a group, for example Friends of Friends, which then will see everything listed to the right of that group.

You can further customize these settings by selecting the Customize Settings link at the bottom of the table (refer to Figure 6.3, #2). Facebook presents the Customize Settings page. This page is organized into Things I Share (content from you such as posts or your birthday), Things Others Share (friends commenting on your posts or tagging you in a photo), and Contact Information. Changing the visibility of Contact Information is covered in the next section. To change the visibility of the other two categories, select the drop-down menu next to the setting you want to change and choose from the menu (see Figure 6.6).

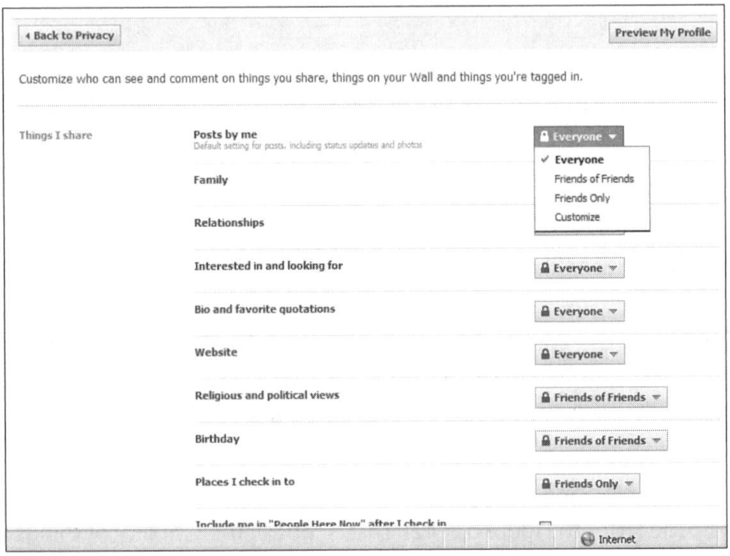

Figure 6.6 *Change privacy settings on the Customize Settings page.*

The menu choices, except Customize, are described in the previous section, "Changing Your Privacy Settings," and are commonly used throughout Facebook. The Customize Setting controls the visibility of this content to specific people or friend lists. If you use Facebook for fun and want to limit what work colleagues can see, you can select all of them by creating a friend list as described in Chapter 4, "Communicating with Your Friends." Then choose Customize (refer to Figure 6.6) and type the name of the friend list in the Hide This From field (see Figure 6.7).

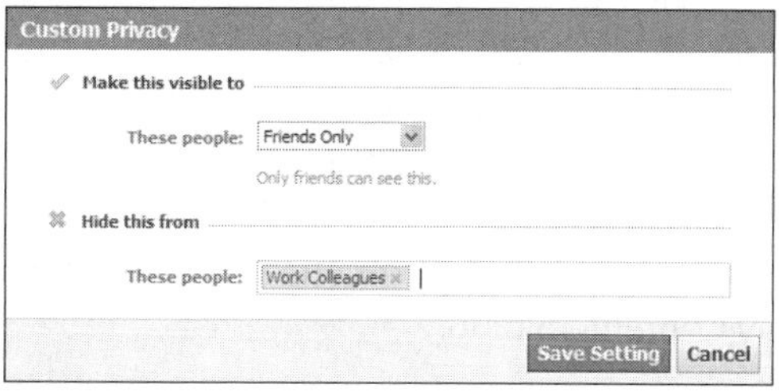

Custom Privacy

Make this visible to

These people: Friends Only

Only friends can see this.

Hide this from

These people: Work Colleagues ×

Save Setting   Cancel

Figure 6.7 *Hide specific content from this friend list using Customize.*

You can also type the names of specific people as well. If you want to make this specific content visible to certain people or a friend list, select Specific People from the drop-down menu titled These People and then type the names of the people and friend lists. Select Save Setting when you are done.

The most restrictive privacy setting is used in case of conflicts. This comes into play if you add the same friend to multiple friend lists and then apply different privacy settings for each friend list.

If you want to check what's visible to certain people after these changes, select Preview My Profile in the upper right and type a friend's name to see your profile as it appears to him or her (refer to Figure 6.5). Select Back to Privacy Settings to return to the main Privacy Settings page.

Control Contact Information Visibility

SHOW ME   Media 6.4—**Control Contact Information Visibility**
Access this video file through your registered Web Edition at
my.safaribooksonline.com/9780132117029/media.

The Sharing on Facebook section also controls who sees your Contact Information. It appears on the table in the middle of the Privacy Settings page (refer to Figure 6.3, #2). As mentioned previously, you might be okay with Facebook's Recommended preset, which makes Contact Information visible to Friends Only (refer to Figure 6.3, see checkmark). This group typically has people you interact with directly.

However, if you want to change the visibility of Contact Information, you could choose one of the presets of Everyone or Friends of Friends, but this changes visibility for several areas. Instead, select the Customize settings link at the bottom of the Sharing on Facebook table. Facebook presents the Customize settings page. Scroll to the bottom, select the drop-down menu next to the Contact Information content you want to control, and choose from the menu (see Figure 6.8). The menu choices are described in the previous section, "Changing Your Privacy Settings," and are commonly used throughout Facebook. The Customize setting is described in "Control Day-to-Day Content Sharing."

Figure 6.8   *Control visibility of contact information using the drop-down menu.*

If you want to see how contact information appears after these changes, scroll to the top and select Preview My Profile in the upper right. Next, type in a friend's name to see how your information appears to him or her (refer to Figure 6.5). Select Back to Privacy Settings to return to the main privacy settings page.

As mentioned previously, the most restrictive privacy setting is used in case of conflicts. For example, if you add the same friend to multiple friend lists, then apply different Contact Information settings for each friend list, the most restrictive view will apply for your friend.

Control What Applications, Games, and Facebook-Enabled Sites Tell Your Friends

 SHOW ME   Media 6.5—Control What Applications, Games, and Facebook-Enabled Sites Tell Your Friends
Access this video file through your registered Web Edition at
my.safaribooksonline.com/9780132117029/media.

Applications, or apps for short, are the little, add-on programs that run inside Facebook. They are akin to a music player running inside of a web browser. Games are just another type of application. Most apps are written by non-Facebook developers and are meant to provide you entertainment, utility, and everything in-between as you interact with friends on Facebook. To learn more about apps, see Chapter 13, "Using Facebook Applications."

For an application to do its job, it needs information about you and your friends. This is okay because you must specifically grant permission to an app before it can access your personal information. Depending on why you joined Facebook, what might not be okay is that your friends can also access your information and see all of your app activity. For example, you may not want your friends to know you ran the "How abnormal am I?" application. So you might want to control what information is open through this back door access. Or you might want to remove apps you no longer use or those that have become spammy.

> Applications can access information available to everyone. This automatically includes your name, profile picture, gender, and networks because the visibility of this information cannot be restricted on Facebook.

The application and Facebook-enabled partner site privacy controls to make adjustments are found in the lower left of the main privacy page (refer to Figure 6.3, #3). When you select the link Edit Your Settings, use the Apps, Games and Websites page (see Figure 6.9) to control the following:

- **Apps you use**—For the installed apps and games shown, you can remove any app by using the Remove link. You can also completely turn off the use of applications by selecting the Turn Off link. By choosing Edit Settings on the right and then Edit Settings next to a specific app, you can see what information it accesses and the time of its last data access. To learn more about applications, see Chapter 13.

- **Info accessible through your friends**—You can customize the profile information and content you post, such as status updates, that are accessible to friends by selecting Edit Settings on the right.

- **Game and app activity**—You can hide your activity using the drop-menu. If you choose Customize from the menu, you can select specific people to show or hide your content from in the same manner shown in "Control Day-to-Day Content Sharing" (refer to Figure 6.7).

- **Instant personalization**—You can enable or disable personalization when you visit any partner website of Facebook by choosing Edit Settings on the right.

- **Public search**—You can enable or disable whether a preview of your profile appears in public search engines. This is described more in the next section.

Figure 6.9 *Use this page to manage access by friends and applications to your information.*

Select the Back to Privacy button at the top of the page to return to the main Privacy Settings page.

Hide from Public Search Engines

 SHOW ME   Media 6.6—Hide from Public Search Engines
Access this video file through your registered Web Edition at
my.safaribooksonline.com/9780132117029/media.

Facebook creates a preview of your profile that displays in public search engines
such as Google, Bing, and Yahoo!. This preview is your photo with basic information
that's visible to everyone (name, gender, and networks) and any other information
you made available to everyone using the Everyone privacy setting described earlier in this chapter. This privacy setting does not hide you from Facebook Search,
which is described in the earlier section, "Control Basic Directory Information Sharing and Facebook Search Visibility" (refer to Figure 6.4).

This setting is found within the Apps and Websites section in the lower left of the
main privacy page (refer to Figure 6.3, #3). Select the link Edit Your Settings, scroll
to Public Search at the bottom, and choose Edit Settings to the right. You can then
be visible to (choose enable) or hide (choose disable) from public search (see
Figure 6.10). You can also preview your profile as a search result by selecting See
Preview.

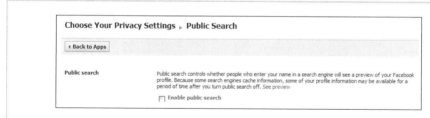

Figure 6.10   *Enable or disable your profile preview in public search engines.*

Select the Back to Apps button at the top of the screen to return to the Apps,
Games, and Website page. Select the Back to Privacy button at the top of that page
to return to the main Privacy Settings page.

Minors—anyone under 18—and their profile previews do not appear in public
search engine results.

Blocking Individual People

 SHOW ME   Media 6.7—Blocking Individual People
Access this video file through your registered Web Edition at
my.safaribooksonline.com/9780132117029/media.

Sometimes a relationship goes astray or someone you friended crosses the line into abuse or harassment. Blocking him or her severs all direct interaction and friendship connections. The person is not notified you blocked him or her and you effectively become invisible to each other on Facebook.

To block someone, select Edit Your Lists from the Privacy Settings page (refer to Figure 6.3, #4). Enter the name or email address of the person you want to block in the appropriate field and select Block This Person or press Enter (see Figure 6.11). To remove someone from your block list, select Unblock next to his or her name. Select the Back to Privacy button to return the main Privacy page.

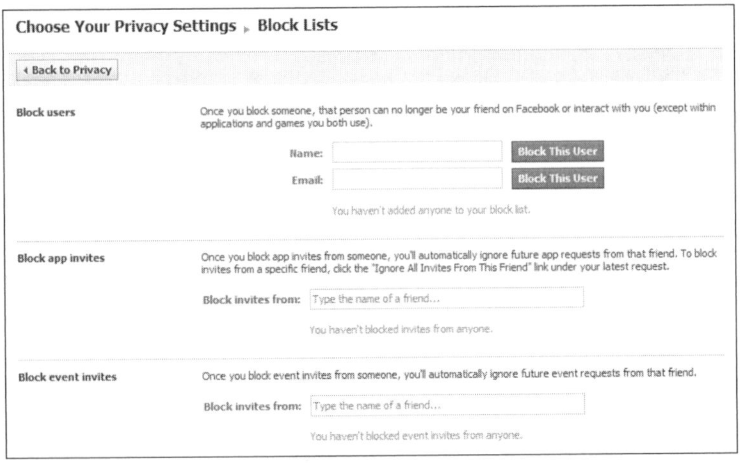

Choose Your Privacy Settings ‣ **Block Lists**

◂ Back to Privacy

Block users   Once you block someone, that person can no longer be your friend on Facebook or interact with you (except within applications and games you both use).

Name: [ ]   Block This User
Email: [ ]   Block This User

You haven't added anyone to your block list.

Block app invites   Once you block app invites from someone, you'll automatically ignore future app requests from that friend. To block invites from a specific friend, click the "Ignore All Invites From This Friend" link under your latest request.

Block invites from: [Type the name of a friend...]

You haven't blocked invites from anyone.

Block event invites   Once you block event invites from someone, you'll automatically ignore future event requests from that friend.

Block invites from: [Type the name of a friend...]

You haven't blocked event invites from anyone.

Figure 6.11   *Enter the name or email address of the person you want to block in the appropriate field.*

If you can't locate the person in the search field, you can block him using his profile page. At the bottom of his page, select the Report/Block This Person link. This same link lets you report a violation, which is covered in the next section.

Reporting Abuse and Violations

 TELL ME MORE   Media 6.8—Reporting Abuse and Violations

Access this video file through your registered Web Edition at
my.safaribooksonline.com/9780132117029/media.

You might run across objectionable or disturbing content given the huge number of people and applications interacting on the site. Facebook wants to know if you find a person or application violating anything in the Statement of Rights and Responsibilities (SRR). Some examples of violations are abusive behavior, compromised profiles, imposter profiles, child exploitation, suicidal content, and terrorist activity or support. Please email abuse@facebook.com to flag the abuse or use the report links available on every profile, photo, message, event, and page. And you can take other steps such as blocking people, as described earlier.

This chapter can't cover all of the continually evolving threats to your privacy and security. If there's something this chapter hasn't addressed, select Help at the bottom of any page, and then Security.

This chapter shows you the different ways to publish your photos and albums on Facebook, and the concept of tagging.

7

Publishing Photos

TELL ME MORE Media 7.1—An Introduction to Publishing Photos
Access this audio recording through your registered Web Edition at
my.safaribooksonline.com/9780132117029/media.

You've posted pictures about a great vacation or looked admiringly at friend's photo album showing his or her new deck at their house. Words are great, but pictures are better! Pictures allow you to post interesting and funny things, without having to describe them. Many families join Facebook, just to share pictures and keep up to date with grandchildren, nieces, and nephews. A family can stay connected even if they are miles apart or can't make certain events.

You should keep certain guidelines in mind when posting a photo. It must be must be 4 megabytes (MB) in size or smaller and cannot be illegal, such as copyrighted, or considered immoral by Facebook. See Facebook's Terms of Service for details (www.facebook.com/terms.php).

Facebook uses albums to hold photos, even if there's just one. Every picture that you upload to Facebook is placed into an album based on either personal preferences or default actions from Facebook. Each photo can have comments and be edited, such as flipping it from portrait to landscape. Others can also comment on the photo. You can also tag people in the photo, which means associating a part of it, typically a face, to a Facebook friend. Tagging has two basic functions. It identifies a person within a photo. It also notifies the person in the photo that a photo has been uploaded of them and shows their recently tagged photos in their profile. Learn more about tagging later in this chapter.

We first cover viewing photos and then posting your own.

Viewing Photos

Facebook gives you a variety of ways to view your photos. One of the most direct approaches is selecting the Photos link under your profile picture from your Profile page. You might also see a row of photos at the top of your profile. These are photos you've been identified, or tagged using Facebook parlance, in.

Facebook also provides numerous ways to see your friends' photos and albums. The most straightforward approach is viewing them as they appear in your News Feed (see Figure 7.1).

Figure 7.1   *Photos in your News Feed from a friend.*

Another way to view photos and albums is by going a friend's Profile page. Similar to your Profile page, a photo strip appears under her name showing the five most recent photos she was tagged in. Also on her profile, you can select one directly from her mini-feed or select the Photos link in the left-side pane to see each album's cover page photo. See Figure 7.2 for an example of photo albums on a friend's profile page.

The consolidated place to view all your and your friend's photos and albums is the Photos page. To get there, select Photos from the left-side pane on your Home page (see Figure 7.3). Here, you can sort by category and upload your own photos.

Figure 7.2   *Photos in your News Feed from a friend.*

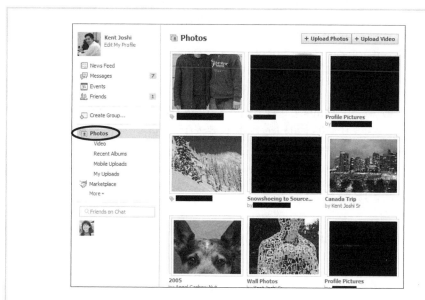

Figure 7.3   *The Photos page consolidates photos from you and your friends in one place.*

Here's what each of the categories does under Photos:

- **Videos**—Select this to show your friend's recently posted videos. To learn more, see Chapter 8, "Publishing Videos."

- **Recent Albums**—Select this to display your friend's recently posted albums.

- **Mobile Uploads**—Select this to see photos uploaded by friends from their mobile device or cell phone. To learn more, see Chapter 9, "Your Mobile Access to Facebook."

- **My Uploads**—Select this to see your photo uploads.

Posting Photos

As you probably know, many people use Facebook to keep their photos. You have three ways to post a single photo to Facebook using its application, called Publisher. The first and most direct is to upload a photo from your computer. The second option is to upload via a special email address. The third option is to take a picture using webcam. We discuss these approaches in the following sections.

Uploading a Photo Using Your Drive or Email

When you upload a photo using these methods, it posts to your Wall, News Feed, your friends' News Feeds (depending on privacy options), and an album. Photos that are uploaded using your drive are automatically placed in the Wall Photo album for easy access later. Photos posted via email are placed in the Mobile Uploads album. You can move a photo to another album once it has been uploaded.

 SHOW ME   Media 7.2—Upload a Photo Using Your Drive or Email
Access this video file through your registered Web Edition at
my.safaribooksonline.com/9780132117029/media.

 LET ME TRY IT

Upload a Photo Using Your Drive or Email

The directions that follow show how to post a single photo on your Wall. It's a quick method to post a photo and add a caption.

1. Select Home from the blue menu bar in the upper right.

2. Select the Photo icon at the top (see Figure 7.4).

Figure 7.4   *Select the Photo icon to open the upload menu.*

3. Select Upload a Photo (see Figure 7.5).

Figure 7.5 *Select Upload a Photo to upload it from your drive.*

4. Select the Browse button to find the photo on your computer and select the photo you want to upload (see Figure 7.6).

Figure 7.6 *Select Browse to open a window to find your photo.*

5. Enter an optional caption in the text box Say Something About This Photo.

6. Facebook defaults to making the photo visible to everyone. If you want to change the privacy settings that control who can see it, select the Lock icon.

7. Click the Share button.

You might have noticed a small link called Upload Via Email. You can see it in Figure 7.6. This link displays instructions on how to upload a picture through email. You are shown a special email address to send your photo to. It was designed for mobile devices but can be used by any device, such as a desktop PC, that can send email. There are also instructions for changing, or refreshing in Facebook language, your upload email address to a different one. You cannot use the old email address after you've refreshed it.

Posting a Photo Taken by a Webcam

Another option to upload photos onto Facebook is through your webcam. This is typically a device that is connected via a USB connection or in some cases included as a built-in device for your laptop. Facebook automatically detects whether you have installed a web camera.

The results from taking a photo using a webcam are similar to uploading a photo from your drive or email. A webcam photo posts to your Wall, News Feed, your friends' News Feeds (depending on privacy options), and the Wall Photos album. You can move the photo to another album once it has been posted.

 SHOW ME   Media 7.3—Post a Photo Taken by a Webcam
Access this video file through your registered Web Edition at
my.safaribooksonline.com/9780132117029/media.

 LET ME TRY IT

Post a Photo Taken by a Webcam

The directions that follow show how to take a photo with your webcam and post it on your Wall. It's a quick method to take a picture and add a caption.

1. Select Home from the blue menu bar in the upper right.

2. Select the Photo icon at the top (refer to Figure 7.4).

3. Select Take a Photo (see Figure 7.7).

Figure 7.7   *Select Take a Photo to capture and post a photo from your webcam.*

4. If prompted, select Allow so Facebook can use your camera and micro-phone—your webcam should activate. Select Close to remove the dialog box (see Figure 7.8).

5. Choose an optional filter effect, such as blur, from the drop-down menu in the upper left. Then select the camera icon at the bottom of the displayed image to take picture. Facebook counts down—3, 2, 1—and then displays the photo.

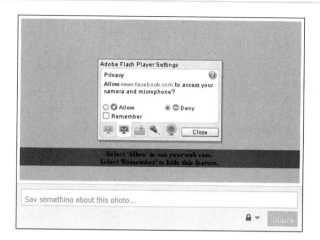

Figure 7.8   *Select Allow to use your webcam to take a photo.*

6. To share the picture, type an optional comment in the text box Say Something About This Photo, change the privacy option using the Lock icon, and select the Share button, as shown at the bottom of Figure 7.8.

> To delete a webcam photo without posting it, select the X in the upper right.

Changing and Sharing Photos

Once you've posted your photos, you can edit and share them with your friends. Perhaps you want to flip a picture so it's not lying on its side, change your profile picture to something else, or add a caption to better describe the picture to your friends. Speaking of your friends, you can comment on their photos, share them with other friends, and download their photos in high resolution if available.

One of the best photo features Facebook is known for is tagging. *Tagging* is when you identify yourself or a friend in a picture. Tagging is simple and is described in this section.

Working with Your Photos

To make changes or share one of your photos, select Photos from the left-side pane on your Profile Page. Then select an album title. When you see the row of photos from your album, select the photo you want to work with.

You can move from photo to photo by selecting the Previous and Next links above the photo. The following lists the different actions that can be performed against each photo (see Figure 7.9):

- **Sharing**—You can share a photo by clicking the Share link located directly below the right side of the photo.

- **Caption**—The caption of the photo is located in the bottom left of the photo. It can be edited by clicking the pencil icon.

- **Tagging**—A person can be tagged in the photo by clicking the Tag This Photo link below the photo on the right.

- **Untagging**—If listed, a person can be untagged in the photo by clicking the Remove Tag link below the photo and on the left.

- **Rotating**—A photo can be rotated 90 degrees in either direction by clicking the arrows in the lower right of the page.

- **Like/Unlike**—Select Like or Unlike below the photo on the left.

- **Commenting**—Comments of the photo are shown underneath the caption of the photo. You can delete any comment that appears under the photo by selecting the X that appears when hovering over the comment.

Figure 7.9 *Editing a photo.*

- **Deleting**—The photo can be deleted from the album by selecting the Delete This Photo link.

- **Editing**—The Edit This Photo link brings you to the album editing page, but only for the single photo. The photo is smaller, but you can see the caption and the people tagged within the photo to the left of the photo. This is described later in the chapter.

- **Make Profile Picture**—Select this link to make the photo your profile picture.

- **Share with Anyone**—The Share This Photo with Anyone link at the bottom of the page opens a new email and pastes a link to the photo in it. You can accomplish the same task by manually copying and pasting the "http:" link into an email (see Figure 7.10).

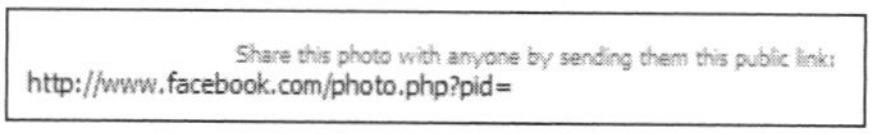

Share this photo with anyone by sending them this public link:
http://www.facebook.com/photo.php?pid=

Figure 7.10   *Share this photo using the public link from Facebook.*

Liking, Sharing, and Downloading Your Friends' Photos

To work with your friends' photos, go to Photos page. To get there, select Photos from the left-side pane on your Home page. Then select an album title from the Photos page. When you see the row of photos from your album, select the photo you want to work with.

You can move through photos in their albums using the Previous and Next links above the photo. Below the photo are options for liking, commenting, and down-loading the photo. Here's what each of those options does (see Figure 7.11):

- **Like/Unlike**—Select this link to give positive feedback or to indicate you enjoyed a photo without leaving a comment. Your like is noted under the photo, a comment is posted to your Wall that you liked your friend's photo, and your friend gets a notification. You can stop liking a photo by selecting the Unlike link.

- **Comment**—If you have permission, select this link or just start typing in the text box titled Write a Comment. The comment can be seen by anyone who sees the image.

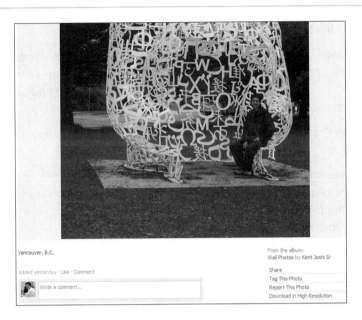

Vancouver, B.C.

From the album:
Wall Photos by Kent Joshi Sr

Added yesterday · Like · Comment

Share
Tag This Photo
Report This Photo
Download in High Resolution

Write a comment...

Figure 7.11   *Working with a friend's photo.*

- **Share**—Select this to share this photo in a few ways. You can share it with all your friends by posting it to your profile or you can share it with specific friends by selecting Send as a Message instead. You can also write a note in the What's on Your Mind text box, and that note appears on your friend's News Feed and your Wall (see Figure 7.12). The Lock icon menu controls whom you share this photo with using Facebook's commonly used groups. These menu options are described in Chapter 6, "Safeguarding Your Information on Facebook." Note, the Share link does not override the privacy settings made by the album owner—photos with strict privacy settings cannot be viewed by friends who don't have permission.

- **Tag This Photo**—Select this to identify a friend in a photo. If the photo owner is not a friend, he or she needs to approve the tag. This is described later in the chapter (refer to Figure 7.10).

- **Report This Photo**—Select this to flag a photo to Facebook.

- **Download in High Resolution**—If available, select this to download the photo as a better quality, high-resolution file. A high-resolution file is larger than a regular-resolution file and takes longer to download.

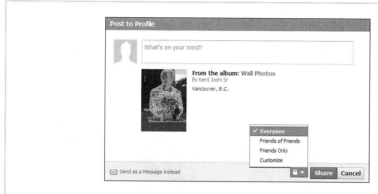

Figure 7.12   *Share the photo using this dialog box.*

Tagging Photos

Photo tagging is when you identify you and your friends in a picture. It's useful to label everyone in a group photo or if you can't see faces clearly. A tagged photo of your friend shows up in the Photo section of his or her profile. Your friend's five most recently tagged photos also appear at the top of his or her profile. If you are tagging a photo that wasn't posted by a friend, then the photo owner needs to approve your tag.

 SHOW ME   Media 7.4—Tag a Person in a Photo
Access this video file through your registered Web Edition at
my.safaribooksonline.com/9780132117029/media.

 LET ME TRY IT

Tag a Person in a Photo

The directions that follow show how to tag a person in a photo that you or a friend uploaded:

1. Open the photo you want to tag.

2. Scroll down past the photo and select the Tag This Photo link.

3. Select the person you want to identify in the photo with your mouse pointer.

4. Select a name or type it in the Tag Name box (see Figure 7.13). If the person doesn't have a Facebook Profile, you can type in a name and optionally include an email address for them to receive a link to the photo.

Figure 7.13 *Type or select someone's name to tag them in this picture.*

5. Select Tag.

6. When are you through identifying everyone in the photo, select Done Tagging above the photo.

You can "untag" yourself from a photo by going to the photo, finding your name, and selecting Remove Tag.

If the photo is offensive or should be removed, select the Report This Photo link.

Creating and Organizing Albums

All photos end up in an album. An album can hold just one or up to 200 photos. You can create as many albums as you want. Each album is a collection of photos grouped by a common factor. Photos can be grouped based on the contents of the photos (such as family vacation) or by access (for example, Everyone, Family, and Friends Only). More information on privacy settings can be found in Chapter 6.

Creating a Photo Album

Uploading one photo at a time gets tedious when you have many photos from a vacation or an event. This is where creating a photo album becomes useful. If you create an album using Facebook Publisher, it asks about the album name, location, resolution or quality, and privacy settings.

Facebook has two applications to upload your photos. The newer one is called the Advanced Uploader—you hold the Control button to select multiple photos. The advanced uploader can handle a photo file up to 15MB in size using the .jpg, .gif, .bmp, or .png formats. The older one, called Simple Uploader, requires you to browse and select each file individually. It can handle a file size up to 4MB.

 SHOW ME   Media 7.5—Create a New Photo Album
Access this video file through your registered Web Edition at
my.safaribooksonline.com/9780132117029/media.

 LET ME TRY IT

Create a New Photo Album

The directions that follow show how to create a new album without editing. The album is created by uploading photos from your drive using the Advanced Uploader. It's a quick method to create an album, add information, and adjust resolution and privacy settings.

1. From your Home Page, select the Photo icon at the top of the page.

2. Select Create an Album (see Figure 7.14).

Figure 7.14   *Select Create an Album to create one by uploading photos from your drive.*

3. Click Select Photos to open a window to select the photos you want to upload. As mentioned, hold down the Control button on your PC to upload multiple photos at once (see Figure 7.15).

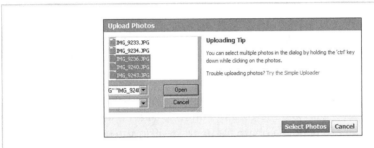

Figure 7.15   *Click Select Photos to see a window to select the photos you want to upload.*

4. After selecting your photos, select Open to upload them.

If you are having problems uploading using the Advanced Uploader, you can try the Simple Uploader (refer to Figure 7.15).

5. While your photos are being uploaded, you can fill in an album name, location, and change the photo quality. You can also change privacy settings by selecting the Lock icon. Select Create Album when you are done filling in album information (see Figure 7.16).

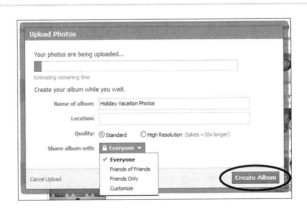

Figure 7.16   *Fill in album information and select Create Album when you are done.*

6. To post your photos and album information as is, select Publish Now (see Figure 7.17). The next section covers editing the photo and album information.

Figure 7.17   *Select Publish Now to post your album as is.*

You can also upload photos to a new album by selecting Photos from the left-side pane of your Home or Profile page. You might need to select More to make the Photos button visible on your Home page. Then select Upload Photos from the upper right. Both approaches use the Advanced Uploader.

Editing and Organizing Your Albums

Once an album has been uploaded to Facebook, it can be changed, shared, commented on, tagged, and also deleted—all in Facebook. You can see your albums by selecting Photos under your Profile picture from your Profile page. After selecting an album title, here's a list of the actions you can take when you see the thumbnail view of photos in your album (see Figure 7.18):

You can edit and change only albums you have uploaded. You do not have access to other people's albums, even if you are tagged in one of their photos.

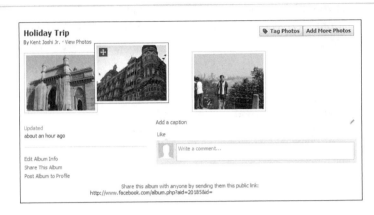

Figure 7.18   *Editing an album from the thumbnail view.*

- **Tag Photos**—In the upper right, select this to tag your friends in these photos.

- **Add More Photos**—Also in the upper right, select this to upload more photos to this album.

- **Change Order of Photos**—Select and drag a photo to a new spot (refer to middle photo in Figure 7.18).

- **Edit Album Info**—From the left side menu, select this link to change album information, privacy, and other settings. This is described later in the chapter.

- **Share This Album**—Also from the left side menu, select this link to share this album through Facebook messaging.

- **Post Album to Profile**—Post the album to your profile by selecting this link from the menu on the left.

- **Add a Caption**—In the middle of the page, select this link, or the pencil icon to the right, and type in an album caption in the text box. Select Save when you are done.

- **Like/Unlike**—Select Like or Unlike from the middle of the page.

- **Comment**—Type a comment for this album in the text box titled Write a Comment.

- **Share Album with Anyone**—Selecting this link automatically pastes a link to the album in a new email. You can also manually copy the "http:" link at the bottom of the page into an email to share it.

To edit album details, select Edit Album Info from the menu in the lower left (refer to Figure 7.18).

You can also edit album details starting from your Home page. Select Photos under your Profile picture, then the Edit Album link under the album you want to change. You may need to choose a submenu under Photos, such as My Uploads, to find your album.

Now that you've opened an album in edit details mode, the following is a list of the actions you can take from the Edit Photos tab (see Figure 7.19):

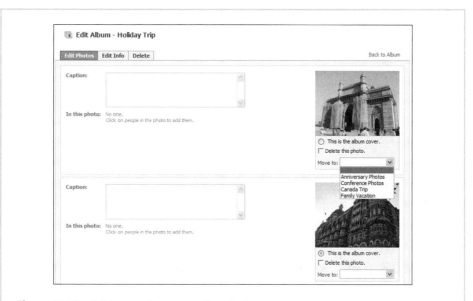

Figure 7.19 *Editing an album using the Edit Photos tab.*

- **Caption**—Add a photo caption by typing in the text box.
- **Tagging**—Tag someone by clicking on him or her in the photo.
- **Album Cover**— Change the album cover to this photo by selecting This is the album cover button under the photo.
- **Delete a Photo**—Checkmark Delete this photo under the photo to remove it from the album.

- **Move to another Album**—Select the new album name from the Move to drop-down menu under the photo (refer to open drop-menu in Figure 7.19).

- **Back to Album**—Select this to return to the thumbnail view of photos in the album. Note, this exits editing without saving changes.

When you are finished making changes, scroll down and select Save Changes.

If you select the Edit Info Tab, here's a list of the actions from that page (see Figure 7.20). When you are finished making changes, be sure to select Save Changes.

Figure 7.20   *Editing an album using the Edit Info tab.*

- **Album Name, Location, Description**—Type in the respective text box to change these.

- **Privacy**—Select the visibility of the album from the drop-down menu with the Lock icon. See Chapter 6 for details about working with Facebook's privacy settings.

- **Share Album with Anyone**— Selecting this link automatically pastes a link to the album in a new email. You can also manually copy the "http:" link at the bottom of the page into an email to share it.

- **Back to Album**— Select this to return to the thumbnail view of photos in the album. Note, this exits editing without saving changes.

If you select the Delete tab (refer to Figure 7.20), you are prompted to delete the entire album.

This chapter explores how to view a video, record a video from your webcam, upload an already recorded video, and edit a video after it is on Facebook.

8

Publishing Videos

Facebook uses video as another way to communicate with your friends. You can share live action footage of a school play, watch a movie trailer, or just send a quick video message to say "Hi!" Videos provide a new level of communication. A benefit of Facebook videos is the ability to leave video messages that friends and family can view at their convenience. This is useful, for example, for business travelers who travel to different time zones. Facebook is one of the few social networks that stores videos to view as another way to communicate.

Facebook also supports high-quality (HQ) video clips. This means you can upload videos at better resolution, as much as 1280 by 720 pixels (720p), resulting in crisper quality. Even if you don't upload HQ videos, you can still watch them on Facebook.

You should keep certain guidelines in mind when working with a video. It cannot be more than 1024 megabytes (MB) in size or 20 minutes in length. It should contain personal content, not commercial or copyrighted content, and cannot be considered immoral by Facebook. See Facebook's Terms of Service for details (www. facebook.com/terms.php).

We'll first cover viewing a video and then posting and editing one.

 TELL ME MORE   Media 8.1—An Introduction to Publishing Videos
Access this audio recording through your registered Web Edition at
my.safaribooksonline.com/9780132117029/media.

Viewing a Video

Similar to photos, Facebook gives you a variety of ways to view videos. You can see your uploaded videos or those you've been tagged, or identified, in. A direct approach is from your Profile page—select the Photos link under your profile picture and then See All Videos, for your uploaded videos, or View Videos of You, for videos you're tagged in (see Figure 8.1).

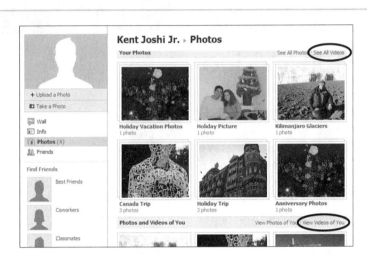

Figure 8.1   *Choose See All Videos or View Videos of You to view your videos.*

When you see the video you want to watch, click the picture. Facebook displays another window with video loaded. Click the picture again, and it starts playing.

When you hover your mouse over the bottom of the video, you see these player controls (see Figure 8.2):

- **Play/Pause**—Select this to pause the video when it's playing. Select it again to play the video from where you paused it.

- **Timeline**—Select a spot on the timeline, which is next to Play/Pause, to advance or go back to a certain spot in the video.

- **Sound**—Select the speaker icon to silence or unsilence the sound. You can adjust the video's volume by clicking and dragging next to the speaker icon.

- **High Quality**—Select the HQ button to switch between high-quality or regular-quality video. The video may reload when switching.

- **Full-screen**—Select the rectangle on the far right of the control bar to switch to full-screen mode. Press the Esc key on PCs to turn off full-screen viewing.

You may see options to Tag, Share, and do other things with the video beneath the view screen. These are described later in this chapter.

Figure 8.2   *Use the player controls beneath the video to view your videos.*

You can also view your friends' videos. You can find them in your News Feed as they post them. You can also select the video link under your profile picture from your Home page (see Figure 8.3).

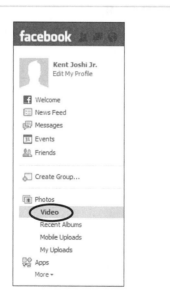

Figure 8.3   *Select Video to see a list of your friends' videos.*

Uploading a Video

Now that you've seen some videos, it's time to talk about how to post your own. Similar to the options for photo uploads, you can upload a video from your computer, through email, or using a webcam. However, unlike photos, the video posting process isn't immediate. A video requires conversion into another format, called encoding, which is time on top of the time to upload.

Uploading a Video from Your Drive

The easiest way to post a video on Facebook is to upload it from your drive. If you want to upload a video from another site, such as YouTube, you need to post a link to it using the Link icon from your Profile page.

SHOW ME   Media 8.2—Upload a Video from Your Drive
Access this video file through your registered Web Edition at
my.safaribooksonline.com/9780132117029/media.

LET ME TRY IT

Upload a Video from Your Drive

The following steps show you how to upload a video that has been stored on your computer and place it on Facebook:

1. Select Home from the blue menu bar in the upper right.

2. Select the Photos link beneath your profile picture (see Figure 8.4). You may need to select More to see the menu option.

3. Select + Upload Video from the upper right (see Figure 8.5).

4. The Upload screen defaults to the File Upload tab. Select the Browse button to find the video on your computer and select the video you want to upload (see Figure. 8.6).

You need to have a Facebook verified account to upload the maximum video sizes allowed by Facebook (refer to Figure 8.6). If you don't, your video is limited to 100 MB and under two minutes.

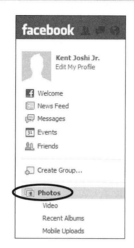

Figure 8.4   *Select Photos to see the Photos page.*

Figure 8.5   *Select + Upload Video to open the Upload screen.*

Figure 8.6   *Select Browse to open a window to find your video.*

5.   You can fill in optional information while your video is uploading. Enter friends' names in the In This Video field to tag them. Enter a title and description in the corresponding fields. Facebook defaults to making the video visible to everyone. If you want to change the privacy setting for this video, select the Lock icon.

6. Select the Save Info button when you are through entering information. Because a video can take anywhere from a few minutes to several hours to upload, you don't need to wait for it to complete before clicking Save Info.

7. You can check Notify Me and Facebook will let you know when it finishes processing and encoding your video (see Figure 8.7).

Figure 8.7   *Check Notify Me so Facebook can contact you when your video has finished processing.*

Facebook will notify you through email of any upload or encoding errors.

Uploading a Video via Email

You can also upload videos to Facebook anywhere you have email. This means you can post videos immediately after capturing them, whether you're on Facebook or not.

This is called Mobile Videos. A unique email address is associated with your account. Any video sent to this address is immediately posted to your wall and sent out to your friends' News Feeds. You can write a caption for the video using the email's subject line and edit it later in Facebook. A single caption is applied if multiple videos are attached to the email.

Because it does not matter who uses the email address, you should think about privacy when using mobile uploads. First, consider guarding who knows your unique upload address. Also, a mobile upload of a video defaults to visible by everyone, but you can change this on your Photos page.

Your address can be found by selecting the Mobile Video tab (refer to Figure 8.6). Write down what's displayed or select the Send the Upload Email for My Page to Me Now link for options to email or text the address to you.

If you want to change the upload email for your account, select Refresh Your Upload Email link within the Mobile Video tab. Once you've refreshed your address, you will not be able to use your old one.

> The email provided is the same email address for uploading photos remotely, as seen in Chapter 7, "Publishing Photos." When you refresh your special upload email address in either Photos or Videos, it is changed for the other also.

 SHOW ME Media 8.3—Uploading a Video via Email
Access this video file through your registered Web Edition at
my.safaribooksonline.com/9780132117029/media.

Uploading a Video Recorded by a Webcam

Recording a video allows you to directly post a video to Facebook. Facebook provides different ways to use the Video application. You can post a short video message to your wall, to a Facebook message, add it to an event, or you can just publish it.

The prerequisites for recording video on Facebook are a webcam, microphone, and the latest Adobe Flash Player. A webcam is typically a device connected via a USB connection or in some cases an expansion card to either your laptop or desktop. Facebook automatically detects whether you have installed a web camera.

The same restrictions that apply to an uploaded video apply to a recorded video. The video must be 20 minutes or 1024 MB in size or smaller. It must also conform to Facebook's Terms of Service (www.facebook.com/terms.php).

 SHOW ME Media 8.4—Upload a Video Recorded by a Webcam
Access this video file through your registered Web Edition at
my.safaribooksonline.com/9780132117029/media.

 **LET ME TRY IT**

Upload a Video Recorded by a Webcam

The directions that follow show how to record a video with your webcam. It's one method to record a video, add information, and tag your friends. Because you are posting using a webcam, Facebook automatically tags you in the video.

1. Select Home from the blue menu bar in the upper right.

2. Select the Photos link beneath your profile picture.

3. Select + Upload Video from the upper right.

4. Select the Record Video tab (see Figure 8.8).

Figure 8.8   *Select the Record Video tab to record a video using your webcam.*

You need to have a Facebook verified account to upload the maximum video sizes allowed by Facebook. If you don't, your recorded video is limited to 100 MB and under 2 minutes.

5. If prompted, select Allow so Facebook can use your camera and micro-phone—your webcam should activate. Select Close to remove the dialog box (see Figure 8.9).

Figure 8.9   *Select Allow to use your webcam to record a video.*

6. Select the red and white button at the bottom to begin recording (see Figure 8.10).

Figure 8.10   *Select red and white button at the bottom to begin recording.*

7. Facebook displays remaining time left in the upper left. Select the button at the bottom to stop recording (see Figure 8.11).

Figure 8.11   *Select the white button at the bottom to stop recording.*

8. To replay, select the play triangle. You can record over again by selecting Reset. If you are happy with the video, select Save (see Figure 8.12).

Figure 8.12 *Use the controls at the bottom to replay, save, or reset to re-record your video.*

9. After selecting Save, choose a thumbnail from the right, fill in as many fields as you want, change privacy settings using the Lock icon, and select Save to post. If you want to delete the video, select Delete. If you want to fill in details later without publishing, select Skip for Now (see Figure 8.13).

Figure 8.13 *Fill in as many fields as you want and use the buttons at the bottom to edit or delete your video.*

If you have issues with your webcam, verify Adobe Flash Player is the latest version. To do this, right-click anywhere on the screen where a webcam image should show, such as the grey area in Figure 8.9, then select About Adobe Flash Player from the menu. When the Adobe website loads, scroll and find two tables. One displays your installed version of Adobe Flash player. Compare your installed version with the second table that displays the latest version available.

Send a Video in a Facebook Message

You can attach video captured by your webcam in a Facebook message. This is useful if you want to send a private video message to a friend or a share a video with multiple friends.

As before, the prerequisites for recording video on Facebook are a webcam, microphone, and the latest Adobe Flash Player. Facebook automatically detects whether you have installed a web camera.

The same restrictions that apply to an uploaded video apply to a recorded video. The video must be 20 minutes or 1024 MB in size or smaller. It must also conform to Facebook's Terms of Service (www.facebook.com/terms.php).

 SHOW ME   Media 8.5—Send a Video Message Recorded by Your Webcam

Access this video file through your registered Web Edition at
my.safaribooksonline.com/9780132117029/media.

 LET ME TRY IT

Send a Video Message Recorded by Your Webcam

The following directions show how to record a video directly to a Facebook Message:

1. Select the messages icon from the blue menu bar, then select Send a New Message (see Figure 8.14).

Figure 8.14   *Select the Messages icon and then Send a New Message.*

2. Type in one or more names of friends you want to receive the video message. Type a subject and message in the appropriate fields.

3. Select the Video icon, which looks like a video camera.

4. If prompted, select Allow so Facebook can use your camera and microphone—your webcam should activate. Select Close to remove the dialog box (refer to Figure 8.9).

5. Select the red and white button at the bottom to begin recording (refer to Figure 8.10).

6. Facebook displays the remaining time left in the upper left. Select the white button at the bottom to stop recording (refer to Figure 8.11).

7. To replay, select Play. You can record over again by selecting Reset. If you are happy with the video and want to send it, select Send (see Figure 8.15).

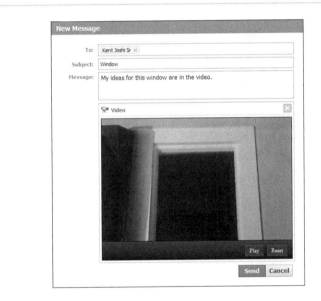

Figure 8.15   *If you are happy with the video, select Send.*

Editing Videos

All videos are eventually published to your profile, but this doesn't necessarily mean that everyone can see them. Your privacy settings work much like the privacy setting for photos. You might see a video posted to your wall, but if you set the privacy setting to Only Me, you are the only one who can see that post. Videos themselves cannot be changed, but how they are presented to Facebook and your friends can be changed. You can take any video and post it to your wall or send it as a message through Facebook Messaging.

One way to edit a video is select Profile from menu at the top and then Photos on the left under your profile picture. Select the See All Videos link (refer to Figure 8.1). Then, select the Edit Video link next to the video you'd like to change (see Figure 8.16).

Figure 8.16   *Select the Edit Video link to open the edit video form.*

In the screen that follows, you can tag your friends and change the title, description, privacy settings, or thumbnail picture for this video. For additional controls, select Cancel (see Figure 8.17).

Figure 8.17   *Change the displayed video using the provided options or select Cancel to move to the next screen.*

You can move to a different video by selecting the Previous and Next links above each video. Most of the controls to edit a video are below it. The following is a list of different options (see Figure 8.18).

Figure 8.18   *Editing a video.*

- **Like/Unlike**—Select this link to give positive feedback or to indicate you enjoyed a video without leaving a comment. Your like is noted under the video, a comment is posted to your Wall that you liked your friend's video, and your friend gets a notification. You can stop liking a video by selecting the Unlike link.

- **Comment**—If you have permission, select this link or just start typing in the text box titled Write a Comment. The comment can be seen by anyone who sees the video.

- **Share**—Select this button to share this video in a few ways. You can share with all of your friends by posting it to your profile or you can share it with specific friends by selecting Send as a Message instead. You can also write a note in the What's on your mind text box and that note appears on your Friend's News Feed and your Wall. The menu from the lock icon controls who you share this video with using Facebook's commonly used groups (see Figure 8.19). These groups are described in Chapter 6, "Safeguarding Your Information on Facebook." Note, the Share link does not override the privacy settings made by the video owner—a video with strict privacy settings cannot be viewed by Facebook users or friends who don't have permission.

- **Rotating**—A video can be rotated 90 degrees in either direction by clicking the arrows.

- **View in Regular/High Quality**—Select this to view in either regular or HQ resolution.

- **Tag This Video**—Select this to identify a friend in the video. If the video owner is not a friend, he or she needs to approve your tag. Tagging is described later in the chapter.

- **Edit This Video**—Select this link to see the Edit Video page (refer to Figure 8.16).

Figure 8.19   *Share the video using this dialog box.*

- **Delete Video**—Select this link to permanently delete this video.

- **Embed This Video**—Select this to copy and paste code to display this video on any website. Your privacy settings are still in play, so if people want to view the video, they must be able to view it on Facebook, or you must open privacy settings so that everyone can view it (see Figure 8.20).

Figure 8.20   *Embed your video on any website by copying this code.*

Tagging Someone in a Video

Just like photo tagging, video tagging is when you identify friends and family in a video. When you tag your friends, a post appears in their News Feeds and Walls. If you tag a video that wasn't posted by a friend, then the video owner needs to approve your tag.

You cannot tag someone in a video who does not have a Facebook account.

SHOW ME   Media 8.6—Tag a Person in a Video

Access this video file through your registered Web Edition at
my.safaribooksonline.com/9780132117029/media.

LET ME TRY IT

Tag a Person in a Video

The directions that follow show how to tag a person in a video that you or a friend uploaded:

1. Select the Photos link, under your profile picture, from your profile page.

2. Select the See All Videos link at the top of your screen.

3. Select the Edit Video link.

4. Select a name or type it in the In This Video field (refer to Figure 8.16).

5. Select Save when you are finished (refer to Figure 8.16).

You can untag yourself from a video by going to the video and selecting the remove tag link next to your name.

This chapter introduces you to Facebook Mobile, the perfect solution for Facebook users on the go.

9

Your Mobile Access to Facebook

More than 200 million Facebook members worldwide use Facebook Mobile, and that number continues to grow rapidly. In addition, more than 200 mobile operators in 60 countries deploy Facebook mobile products, which give you mobile access to Facebook from almost anywhere in the world.

In this chapter, you explore the many features of Facebook Mobile. You can also listen to tips on ways to make the most of your mobile experience with Facebook and watch videos that show you how to customize Facebook Text Messages, download Facebook mobile applications, and customize your Facebook Places privacy settings.

What You Can Do with Facebook Mobile

Although certain things are easier to do on the Facebook website (such as writing long messages), you can perform the vast majority of Facebook tasks from a mobile device when you're on the go.

 TELL ME MORE   Media 9.1—What You Can Do with Facebook Mobile
Access this audio recording through your registered Web Edition at
my.safaribooksonline.com/9780132117029/media.

Facebook Mobile enables you to

- Use Facebook Mobile Web to access Facebook from any phone with an Internet browser.
- Send and receive status updates, wall posts, friend requests, and more via text message.
- Upload photos and videos from your cell phone.
- Use custom Facebook mobile applications for many popular cell phones.
- Receive selected friends' status updates by text message.

To learn more about Facebook Mobile, go to http://www.facebook.com/mobile, shown in Figure 9.1. You must log in to Facebook itself before activating or using any of these features, however.

Figure 9.1   *Facebook Mobile offers several ways to interact with Facebook from a mobile device.*

Something you'll notice on the Facebook Mobile web page is that its content is dynamic. When you first open the page, a specific feature is profiled at the top. Refresh your browser, and another feature is profiled at the top. The options that display below each feature vary depending on whether it's at the top or in one of the boxes at the bottom of the page.

Facebook adds new mobile features and functionality on a regular basis. To keep up with what's new, check out its Facebook "fan" page at http://www.facebook.com/UsingFacebookMobile.

Activating Facebook Mobile

The first step in getting started with Facebook Mobile is to activate your phone for use with Facebook Text Messages. Although you don't need to activate your phone to use every feature of Facebook Mobile, it's a good idea to start with this task, particularly if you're interested in sending or receiving status updates, friend requests, messages, wall posts, and more on your cell phone.

LET ME TRY IT

Activate Facebook Mobile for Your Phone

To activate Facebook Mobile, follow these steps:

1. From the main menu, select Account, Account Settings.

2. On the My Account page, select the Mobile tab. Figure 9.2 shows this tab.

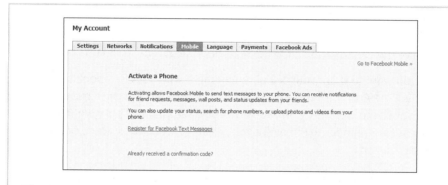

Figure 9.2   *Go to the Mobile tab to get started setting up your phone.*

3. To activate your phone, click the Register for Facebook Text Messages link.

4. In the Activate Facebook Texts (Step 1 of 2) dialog box shown in Figure 9.3, select your country and mobile carrier from the drop-down lists. Then click the Next button.

Figure 9.3   *Select your country and provider to get started.*

5. On your cell phone, send a text message containing the letter "F" (but without the quotation marks) to 32665 (FBOOK) as instructed in the Activate Facebook Texts (Step 2 of 2) dialog box, shown in Figure 9.4.

Figure 9.4 *Step 2 tells you what to do on your cell phone.*

6. Enter the confirmation code that Facebook sends you in the text box.

7. If you want to share your cell phone number with your Facebook friends, select the Add This Phone Number to My Profile check box. Remember that anyone who can view your profile can also see your cell phone number. If you want your number to remain private, clear this check box. Then, click the Next button.

You're now ready to customize the way you use Facebook Text Messages.

Customizing Facebook Text Messages

The Mobile tab on the My Account page now contains many new fields that enable you to customize how you want to use text messaging on Facebook Mobile. This is particularly important if you have many Facebook friends or your friends are very active on the site. You could end up with information overload if you don't specify the exact information you do—and don't—want to receive via text message.

 SHOW ME   Media 9.2—Customizing Facebook Text Messages
Access this video file through your registered Web Edition at
my.safaribooksonline.com/9780132117029/media.

 LET ME TRY IT

Customize Facebook Text Messages for Your Phone

To customize how and when you receive text messages, follow these steps:

1. From the main menu, select Account, Account Settings.

2. On the My Account page, select the Mobile tab. Figure 9.5 shows this tab.

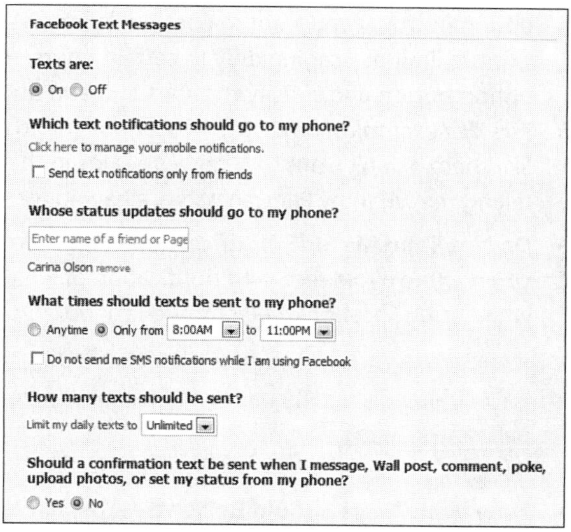

Facebook Text Messages

Texts are:
◉ On ○ Off

Which text notifications should go to my phone?
Click here to manage your mobile notifications.
☐ Send text notifications only from friends

Whose status updates should go to my phone?

Enter name of a friend or Page

Carina Olson remove

What times should texts be sent to my phone?
○ Anytime ◉ Only from 8:00AM ▾ to 11:00PM ▾
☐ Do not send me SMS notifications while I am using Facebook

How many texts should be sent?
Limit my daily texts to Unlimited ▾

Should a confirmation text be sent when I message, Wall post, comment, poke, upload photos, or set my status from my phone?
○ Yes ◉ No

Figure 9.5 *Specify exactly which messages you want to receive and when you want to receive them.*

3. In the Facebook Text Messages section, specify which messages you want to receive and when. Your options include

    • **Texts Are**—By default, text messages are set to on. If you don't want to receive any text messages, select the Off option button. Note that this doesn't affect your ability to send text messages.

    • **Which Text Notifications Should Go to My Phone?**—Click the Click Here link to select which text notifications you want to receive as a text message on your phone. Facebook opens the Notifications tab where you can choose the notifications to receive via SMS (as well as via email). Sample options include receiving a text message when someone sends you a message, adds you as a friend, posts on your Wall, tags you in a photo, tags you in Facebook Places, and more.

    • **Send Text Notifications Only From Friends**—Restrict notifications to activity just from your friends.

    • **Whose Status Updates Should Go to My Phone?**—Enter the names of Facebook friends or pages whose status updates you want to receive. Facebook searches for matches among your friends as you type. Again, you'll want to use this selectively to avoid information overload.

- **What Times Should Texts Be Sent to My Phone?**—Select the Anytime option button if you want to continually receive text messages. If you want to limit messaging only to certain hours, select the Only From option button and specify the start and end times from the drop-down lists. For example, I have many Facebook friends in Europe. As much as I like them, I don't want to receive updates in the middle of the night telling me what my Parisian pals are having for lunch.

- **Do Not Send Me SMS Notifications While I Am Using Facebook**—If you want to avoid receiving notification of what you can see for yourself while using Facebook, select this check box.

SMS stands for Short Message Service, a method used to send text messages between cell phones and websites.

- **How Many Texts Should Be Sent?**—You can receive unlimited messages or limit this amount to a number between 1 and 100 texts per day. Facebook notifies you when you reach your daily limit. If you want to receive more messages, reply to this notification using the word "reset."

- **Should a Confirmation Text Be Sent When I Message, Wall Post, Comment, Poke, Upload Photos, or Set My Status from My Phone?**— If you want to receive confirmation of your own activity, select the Yes option button. Otherwise, select No.

4. Click the Save Preferences button to save your changes.

After you set your initial preferences, you might decide that you're still receiving too many text messages. Or, you might have been too selective and need to receive more information. In either case, you can return to this page at any time to modify the text messages you receive.

Activating Multiple Phones

You can activate Facebook Mobile for more than one phone, but you will receive text messages only on the phone you select in the My Phone section at the bottom of the Mobile tab.

 **LET ME TRY IT**

Activate Facebook Mobile for an Additional Phone

To activate Facebook Mobile for another phone, follow these steps:

1. From the main menu, select Account, Account Settings.

2. On the My Account page, select the Mobile tab.

3. In the Mobile Phones section, click the Add Another Phone link.

4. Follow the steps in the "Activate Facebook Mobile for Your Phone" section earlier in the chapter to activate this additional phone.

Deactivating a Phone

If you change phone numbers or no longer want to use Facebook Mobile, you can deactivate your phone. To do so, click the Remove link to the right of the phone number you want to deactivate in the Mobile Phones section of the Mobile tab.

Accessing Facebook Mobile Web

If you have a phone with an Internet browser, you can use Facebook Mobile Web to update, view, and manage your Facebook account. To access Facebook Mobile Web, navigate to http://m.facebook.com on your cell phone. Figure 9.6 shows an example of Facebook Mobile Web on the iPhone.

Figure 9.6   *Go to m.facebook.com on your cell phone to access Facebook on the go.*

Although Facebook doesn't charge to use Facebook Mobile Web, you're still responsible for any associated data access charges from your mobile carrier.

When you log on to Facebook Mobile Web, you can perform many common Facebook tasks such as viewing your requests, updating your status, and viewing events and your News Feed. Using the top and bottom navigation links, you can access other areas of Facebook. For example, the top menu includes the following options: Home, Profile, Friends, and Inbox. From the Bookmarks section at the bottom of the page, you can access the following: Notifications, Groups, My Pages (if you have at least one Facebook page), Events, Photos, and More.

In addition to using Facebook Mobile Web, also check to see whether there's a mobile application specific to your phone. These custom applications often offer even more features. For more information, see "Using a Custom Facebook Application for Your Phone" later in this chapter.

If you live in one of many supported countries, you could have access to 0.facebook.com, a new mobile site that lets you log on to Facebook from a mobile device without data fees. At present, the United States and Canada aren't on the list, but Facebook adds new countries regularly.

Sending Text Messages

It's easy to send a status update to Facebook when you're on the go. Just send a text message to 32665 (FBOOK) from your activated cell phone. For example, you could text "Having dinner at a great Italian restaurant by the beach" to 32665, and this text will appear as your latest Facebook status. Remember, your mobile carrier's text messaging rates do apply.

If you're unable to send a text message from an activated phone, verify that your message doesn't contain a signature, which can interfere with Facebook Mobile Texts. Also, verify that your mobile plan enables you to send text messages.

If you're looking to do more with text messages, Facebook offers some advanced options. Table 9.1 lists several examples of how you can send private messages, search, post on a friend's wall, and send friend requests via text message.

In the second column, the bolded text refers to the text message command you need to enter, the regular text is an example of the specific Facebook member you want to message or search for (in this case, Anne Smith), and the italicized text is an example of the message you could send this person.

Table 9.1 Facebook Text Messaging Options

To do the following:	Send this via text message on your cell phone:
Message a specific person	**msg** anne smith *hello*
Search for a friend	**search** anne smith
Find a cell phone number	**cell** anne smith
View a list of your current events	**event**
Post something on a friend's wall	**wall** anne smith *congrats!*
Send a friend request	**add** anne smith

Sending Photos and Videos from Your Cell Phone

If you enjoy taking photos or videos with your cell phone, you can easily send them to Facebook right from your phone using Facebook's Mobile Uploads feature. Facebook provides a personalized email address to each Facebook member for this purpose.

> You can also use Mobile Uploads to send a status update to Facebook. Just enter your update in the subject line of the email.

 LET ME TRY IT

Send a Photo or Video to Facebook from Your Cell Phone

To send photos or videos from your cell phone, follow these steps:

1. From the main menu, select Account, Account Settings.

2. On the My Account page, select the Mobile tab.

3. In the upper-right corner of the tab, click the Go to Facebook Mobile link.

4. In the Upload via Email section of the Facebook Mobile page (see Figure 9.7), locate your personal upload email address, such as samplemail@m. facebook.com. This email is associated with your Facebook account, so don't share it with others.

Upload via Email

Use a personalized upload email to post status updates or send photos to your profile. Your personal email is:

Send me my upload email

Your upload email address will display here.

Figure 9.7   *When you're logged in to Facebook, your private upload email address displays on the Facebook Mobile page.*

Optionally, Facebook can send your upload email address to the email address you have listed on the My Account page. To do this, click the Send Me My Upload Email button. This way, you can save this email address as a contact in your email system, ready to use whenever you want to post or upload.

5. On your cell phone, send your photo or video to your personal upload email address, entering an optional caption in the email subject line. The exact steps for performing this task vary by cell phone. If you're unsure, refer to your cell phone's user manual.

Your uploaded photo and videos display on your Facebook profile and News Feed, as shown in Figure 9.8. If you uploaded a photo, you'll also find it in your Mobile Upload photo album. From here, you can edit, tag, or share this photo. You can also modify its privacy settings, which is set to Everyone by default.

Figure 9.8   *View your mobile uploads on your Facebook profile.*

For more information about working with photos and videos on Facebook, see Chapter 7, "Publishing Photos," and Chapter 8, "Publishing Videos."

Changing Your Upload Email Address

If your upload email address is no longer secure, you can change it. For example, you might have accidentally shared it with others or are concerned about the privacy of data on your computer.

 LET ME TRY IT

Request a New Upload Email Address

To receive a new, secure upload email address from Facebook, follow these steps:

1. From the main menu, select Account, Account Settings.

2. On the My Account page, select the Mobile tab.

3. In the upper-right corner of the tab, click the Go to Facebook Mobile link.

4. In the Upload via Email section of the Facebook Mobile page, click the Find Out More link (refer to Figure 9.7).

5. In the Upload Photos via Email dialog box, click the Refresh Your Upload Email link, shown in Figure 9.9.

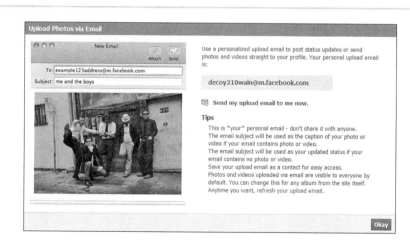

Figure 9.9 *If your private upload email address is no longer secure, request a replacement.*

6. Click the Reset button in the Change Your Personal Upload Email? dialog box to get a new email (see Figure 9.10).

Figure 9.10 *This dialog box verifies that you really want to reset your upload email address before proceeding.*

Using a Custom Facebook Application for Your Phone

Facebook offers special mobile applications for a variety of phones including the following: iPhone (also works with the iPod Touch and iPad), Palm, Sony Ericcson, INQ, BlackBerry, Nokia, Android, Windows Phone, and Sidekick. If your phone isn't on this list, you can still use Facebook Mobile even if there isn't an application specific to your phone.

The functionality of each mobile application varies by phone, but in general you can perform many of the same tasks that are available with Facebook Mobile Web. Some applications also include additional features specific to that phone. For example, the latest Facebook application for the iPhone enables you to watch videos and post on event walls.

SHOW ME   Media 9.3—Downloading Facebook Mobile Applications
Access this video file through your registered Web Edition at my.safaribooksonline.com/9780132117029/media.

LET ME TRY IT

Download a Facebook Application for Your Phone

To download a Facebook app for your phone, follow these steps:

1. From the main menu, select Account, Account Settings.

2. On the My Account page, select the Mobile tab.

3. In the upper-right corner of the tab, click the Go to Facebook Mobile link.

4. On the Facebook Mobile page, select the name of your phone in the Facebook for Your Phone section, shown in Figure 9.11.

Figure 9.11   *Select your phone from among the many options.*

Because features on the Facebook Mobile page aren't in a static location, you could find the Facebook for Your Phone section at the top of the page. In this case, you need to select your phone from a drop-down list.

5. The Facebook page for your phone's application opens. Depending on the application, you can either click the Download App button or scan a QR code with your phone. You'll also find other interesting information about this app, such as reviews, videos, photos, discussions, and more. The content you see, however, varies by application. Figure 9.12 shows a sample page for the BlackBerry application.

Figure 9.12 *If you use a BlackBerry, you'll find plenty of useful information about mobile Facebook access on this page.*

Not every application has its own Facebook page. If you select one of these apps, you skip step 5 and go directly to step 6.

6. Download your application from the external site that opens. For example, the iTunes Store site opens if you select iPhone (see Figure 9.13).

Figure 9.13 *Download the Facebook app for the iPhone from the iTunes store for free.*

Using Facebook Places

When you're on the go, you might want to share your travels and daily activities with your Facebook friends. Using Facebook Places, you can easily check in to a physical location and share this information on Facebook. Facebook Places also enables you to see where your friends are. You never know who could be right around the corner from you.

The Facebook Places application is available for the iPhone, Android, and Black-Berry. You can also access Facebook Places by navigating to http://touch.facebook. com on your mobile device.

Checking In on Facebook Places

How you access and check in to Facebook Places varies by device. In general, you should find Facebook Places on your device's Facebook application home screen.

 LET ME TRY IT

Check In on Facebook Places via touch.facebook.com

To check in and share your location via http://touch.facebook.com, follow these steps:

1. Point your browser to http://touch.facebook.com.

2. Tap the Places tab on your mobile device.

3. Tap the Share Location button.

4. Tap the Share Where You Are with Your Friends link. If you've used Face-book Places before, tap the Check In button instead.

5. Facebook displays a list of locations near you. From here, you can:

   • Tap a location on the list.

   • Enter a place name in the Search Nearby Places box and tap the Search button.

   • Tap the Add button to add a new location. Enter a name and description of the new place and then tap the Add button again.

While you're browsing nearby places, be on the lookout for a yellow icon to the right of a place name. This indicates that the location participates in Facebook Deals and offers a special deal to anyone who checks in via Facebook Places. Sample deals include a 20 percent discount at American Eagle Outfitters or two entrees for the price of one at Chipotle restaurants.

6. Optionally, share what you're doing at this location in the What Are You Doing? box.

7. Optionally, tap the Tag Friends with You link to select from a list of your friends.

8. Tap the Check In button.

Facebook displays your location and any friends with you on your profile Wall (see Figure 9.14) and your friends' News Feed. You can click the name of any location or friend to view their Facebook Places page or Facebook profile.

Figure 9.14   *Facebook posts your location and the friends you're with on your profile Wall.*

Checking Out of Facebook Places

If you want to check out of a place you checked into, you have three options:

- On http://touch.facebook.com, go to the Wall post that mentions your Facebook Places check-in, tap the Remove link, and confirm that you want to delete the post.

- On the Facebook website, go to the Wall post that mentions your Facebook Places check-in, click the X (Remove) button to the right of the post, and click the Remove Post button in the Delete Post dialog box.

- On the Facebook application for the iPhone, Android, or BlackBerry, go to the Wall post that mentions your Facebook Places check-in, swipe your finger to the left over the post, and tap the Delete button.

Protecting Your Privacy with Facebook Places

Although sharing your location with friends, family, and coworkers makes it easier to keep track of what everyone is doing, you might not want all of your Facebook friends to know your exact location. By default, Facebook lets your friends know when you check into a place and also enables them to check you in. If Facebook friends include only people you know well, the default settings could offer sufficient privacy. But if your Facebook friends include people you don't know well, you might want to place more restrictions on who knows your location. Fortunately, you can customize your privacy settings with Facebook Places.

 SHOW ME   Media 9.4—Customizing Your Facebook Places Privacy Settings
Access this video file through your registered Web Edition at
my.safaribooksonline.com/9780132117029/media.

 LET ME TRY IT

Customize Your Facebook Places Privacy Settings

To customize your Facebook Places privacy settings, follow these steps:

1. From the main menu, select Account, Privacy Settings.

2. On the Choose Your Privacy Settings page, click the Customize Settings link.

3. In the Places I Check Into field (see Figure 9.15), select one of the following options:
   - **Everyone**—Display your location to everyone on Facebook.
   - **Friends of Friends**—Display your location to your friends and their friends.
   - **Friends Only**—Display your location only to your friends (the default setting).
   - **Customize**—Open the Custom Privacy dialog box where you can limit viewing of your location to specific friends or prevent specific friends from viewing it.

4. In the Include Me in "People Here Now" After I Check In field, select the Enable checkbox (the default setting) if you want your name and photo to display in People Here Now. If you don't want to display your name and photo, remove the checkmark. See Figure 9.16 to view an example of People Here Now.

Figure 9.15   *Specify exactly who can see your location on Facebook.*

Figure 9.16   *By default, Facebook displays your name and photo when you check into a place on Facebook Places.*

People Here Now is a section on a Facebook Places page that displays users who have checked in to that place. This section is visible to friends and others who have checked in nearby.

5. Click the Edit Settings button to the right of the Friends Can Check Me Into Places field (scroll down the page to find this setting).

6. In the Places: Friend Tags dialog box, select Enabled or Disabled from the drop-down list. By default, your friends can check you into Places.

See Chapter 6, "Safeguarding Your Information on Facebook," for more information about Facebook privacy.

10

Joining and Creating Groups

Facebook Groups provide a great way to share information and discuss common
interests with a group of like-minded people on Facebook.

In this chapter, you learn how to find, join, participate in, and create groups. You
can also listen to tips on ways to make the most of your group experience and
watch videos that show you how to search for and join a group, participate in a
group, create your own group, and administer a group you created.

Understanding How Groups Work

A Facebook group is similar to a discussion board or forum. Facebook members
search for and join groups that interest them to connect with others in a focused
environment whose structure is similar to Facebook itself. For example, groups
enable you to share content such as posts, links, photos, and videos, just like you
can on your profile Wall.

Facebook upgraded its group functionality in 2010 to offer many new features
including group chat, a shared notepad, and email notifications. This chapter
covers Facebook's new group functionality. If you find a group that doesn't offer
these new features, the group owner created it before Facebook introduced the
new group design. You can't convert an old group to the new design; you must
start again with a new group.

Figure 10.1 shows an example of a group using Facebook's new group design.

Figure 10.2 shows an example of a group created with Facebook's old group
design, which doesn't include new group features such as sharing docs or participating in group chats.

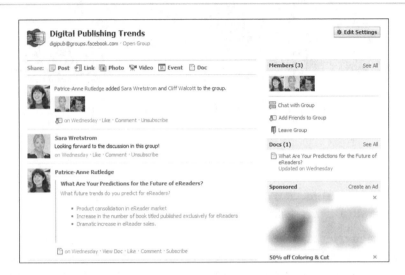

Figure 10.1   *A Facebook group enables you to discuss a common interest with other Facebook members.*

Figure 10.2   *Older Facebook groups still offer a great way to communicate with others, but don't include new group features.*

  TELL ME MORE   Media 10.1—Making the Most of Your Participation in Facebook Groups

Access this audio recording through your registered Web Edition at my.safaribooksonline.com/9780132117029/media.

Facebook offers three types of groups:

- **Open** groups that any Facebook member can view and join. Members and content are public with an open group.

- **Closed** groups that display in group search results but require that members request to join. Members are public with a closed group, but content is private.

- **Secret** groups that are hidden from search results and are available by invitation only. Both members and content are private with a secret group. Secret groups don't appear in search results.

Many Facebook users wonder whether they should create a group or a page. A Facebook group works as a discussion board or forum, whereas a Facebook page is essentially a profile for a business, organization, or public figure. If you're looking for a way to discuss a topic in either a public or private environment, choose a group. If you're looking to promote your business or organization, a page provides more visibility. For more information about Facebook pages, see Chapter 14, "Making Business Connections on Facebook."

Searching for and Joining Facebook Groups

Facebook offers millions of groups for like-minded people interested in discussing and sharing their favorite topics. A quick search offers numerous possibilities. When you find a group you like, it's easy to join.

Facebook allows you to join up to 300 groups. If you reach that limit, you have to leave some of your current groups before you can join more.

 SHOW ME   Media 10.2—Searching for and Joining a Group
Access this video file through your registered Web Edition at
my.safaribooksonline.com/9780132117029/media.

LET ME TRY IT

Search for and Join a Group

To search for and join a Facebook group, follow these steps:

1. Enter the group topic you're searching for in the search box at the top of your Facebook screen and click the Search button (a small magnifying glass).

2. Facebook displays the closest matches to your search term in a drop-down list, shown in Figure 10.3. If you see the group you want, click its title to open it. If you don't see the group you want, click the See More Results link to display all results.

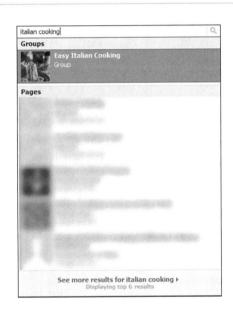

Figure 10.3   *Perform a quick search to find interesting groups to join.*

3. By default, Facebook displays all results for this search term, including people, pages, and groups. To narrow your results only to groups, click the Groups link on the left side of the page.

4. Your search results display each group's name, its type, and its number of members. Figure 10.4 displays sample search results for groups related to "Italian cooking." From this list, you can

Figure 10.4 *Narrow down your results to find the right group.*

- Click the title of a group to view more information about it. If a group has open access, you can view current group activity to determine if this is the right group for you. If a group requires approval before joining, you can view only basic information about the group.

- If the group is an open group, click the Join Group button to the right of the group name to join the group. You can access your group immediately.

- If the group is a closed group, click the Request to Join button to the right of the group name to send a join request. You won't be able to access your group until the group creator or admin approves you as a group member.

The groups you already belong to display at the top of this list and don't include a Join Group or Request to Join button.

Participating in Groups

In many ways, participating in a group is similar to regular participation on Facebook. The center column of each Facebook group includes a group Wall (refer to Figure 10.1), similar to your own profile's Wall. Here you can read the Wall posts of other group members, like the posts that are most relevant to you, add your own comments, and subscribe to posts you want to follow by email.

The Share menu, located at the top of your group Wall, enables you to share content on the group Wall. You can share posts, links, photos, videos, events, and docs. This menu is very similar to the Share menu you see on your home page or profile, with the exception of sharing docs (a shared notepad), which is unique to groups.

For more information on docs, see "Sharing Group Docs" later in this chapter. For a reminder of how to post Wall content, photos, videos, events, and more, refer to the chapters in this book that focus on those topics.

Although most Facebook members join groups to discuss and learn about topics they enjoy, others use Facebook groups as a promotional tool. Sharing your business activities with fellow group members is acceptable in most groups, but you don't want to overdo this. Focus on providing value and becoming part of the community rather than delivering sales pitches to fellow group members.

 SHOW ME   **Media 10.3—Participating in Groups**
Access this video file through your registered Web Edition at
my.safaribooksonline.com/9780132117029/media.

Accessing Your Groups

To access any of the groups you've joined, click the link with the name of your group in the left column of your Facebook home page (see Figure 10.5).

Figure 10.5   *Find your group in the left column of your home page.*

If you don't see a link for the group you want to open, click the See All link at the bottom of the list to open the Groups page. Then, click the title of the group you want to access from the list of groups that displays.

On the Groups page, you can also view a list of groups your friends have requested you join. You can choose to either join or ignore these group invitations.

Sharing Groups with Your Friends

If you join a group that some of your Facebook friends would also enjoy, you can share information about the group with them. For example, you can post a comment and link about a group on your profile or send selected friends a message about that group.

 LET ME TRY IT

Share a Group with Your Friends

To spread the word about a favorite group with your friends, follow these steps:

1. When viewing the group you want to share, scroll down to the bottom of the page and click the Share link (below your group's Wall posts).

2. In the Post to Profile dialog box, shown in Figure 10.6, let your friends know why you recommend this group in the What's on Your Mind text box.

Figure 10.6 *Spread the word about your favorite groups by posting news about them on your profile.*

3. Click the down arrow to the right of the lock icon to select who can see your post. Your choices include Everyone (the default), Friends and Networks, Friends of Friends, Friends Only, or Customize.

If you choose Customize, the Custom Privacy dialog box opens where you can specify exactly who can and can't view your post. Another option is to send a message to specific friends rather than post information on your profile. You can do this by clicking the Send as a Message Instead link that displays on the Post to Profile dialog box.

4. Click the Share button to share this group with other Facebook members based on the criteria you specified.

Editing Group Settings

In the Edit Settings dialog box, you can specify when you want Facebook to notify you about group activity and how often to display a link to a specific group in your home page navigation.

 LET ME TRY IT

Edit Group Settings

To edit group settings, follow these steps:

1. Click the Edit Settings button in the upper-right corner of any group page (refer to Figure 10.1).

2. In the Edit Settings for [Group Name] dialog box, shown in Figure 10.7, specify when Facebook should notify you: when a member posts or comments, when a member posts (the default), when a friend posts, or only for posts you are subscribed to.

Figure 10.7   *Stay in control of when Facebook notifies you about group activity.*

3. By default, the Email Notifications To checkbox is selected and Facebook sends group notifications to the email listed. If you don't want to receive any email about this group, remove this checkmark. To stop receiving all email group notifications, click the Edit Your Notification Settings link and customize your group notifications on the Notifications tab of the My Account page.

4. Specify how often you want Facebook to display this group in the left column of your home page: Always, Sometimes (the default), or Never. If you plan to access this group frequently, choose Always.

5. By default Facebook sends you group chat messages. If you don't want to receive these, remove the checkmark from the Send Me Group Chat Messages checkbox.

6. Click the Save Settings button to save your settings.

Sharing Group Docs

A group doc is a shared notepad where you post and format text that fellow group members are able to read and edit. Think of it as a mini wiki for your Facebook group. Only groups created with Facebook's new group design include this feature.

 LET ME TRY IT

Share a Group Doc

To share a doc on a group's Wall, follow these steps:

1. Click the Doc link on the Share menu to open the notepad (see Figure 10.8).

2. Enter a title for your doc.

3. In the text box, type the text you want to share.

4. Format your text using the buttons that display above the text box. These include
   - Bold
   - Italics
   - Numbered list
   - Bullet list

5. Click the Save button to post your doc, shown in Figure 10.9.

Figure 10.8   *Collaborate on short documents with fellow group members.*

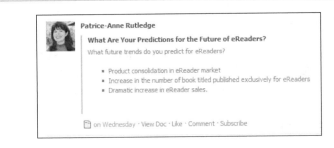

Figure 10.9   *Your formatted doc now displays on your group's Wall.*

Other group members can view and edit your doc, like it, post a comment about it, or subscribe to receive email when someone updates it.

 LET ME TRY IT

Edit a Group Doc

To edit a group doc that you or another group member created, follow these steps:

1. On your group page, click the View Doc link below the posted doc (refer to Figure 10.9).

2. Click the Edit link to the right of the post. Facebook opens the notepad where you can enter and format text. See "Share a Group Doc" earlier in this chapter for more information about formatting options.

3. Click the Save button to save your changes.

Facebook displays your changes as the current version of the doc, shown in Figure 10.10. To scroll through changes other group members have made, use the left and right arrow buttons.

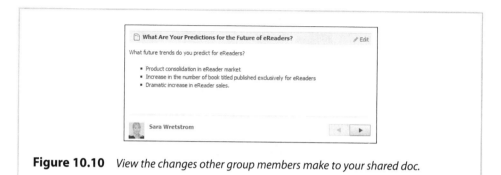

Figure 10.10   *View the changes other group members make to your shared doc.*

Participating in Group Chats

Another feature of Facebook's new group design is the ability to hold group chats. Unlike traditional chat, covered in Chapter 4, "Communicating with Your Friends," group chats enable you to chat with more than one person, but only if they are all members of the same group and are all logged in to Facebook. Group chat is available only for groups of 250 members or less.

 LET ME TRY IT

Participate in a Group Chat

To participate in a group chat, follow these steps:

1. On your group page, click the Chat with Group link in the right column, shown in Figure 10.11.

Figure 10.11   *Group chat is a convenient feature of Facebook's new group design.*

2. Facebook opens the chat window, showing photos of the group members who are currently online (see Figure 10.12). A small green square in the lower left corner of a group member's photo means that this person is active and available to chat. A small blue square means that the person is idle and hasn't been active on Facebook in the last 10 minutes.

Figure 10.12   *Chat with multiple members of your group at the same time.*

3. Type your message in the text box at the bottom of the chat window and press the Enter key. Group chat is very similar to a traditional Facebook chat. For more information about Facebook's chat functionality, see Chapter 4.

Leaving a Group

If you decide you no longer want to participate in a group, you can leave it. To do so, click the Leave Group link in the right column of any group.

If you're leaving a group because of the unprofessional conduct of other group members, you can report this to Facebook by clicking the Report Group link at the bottom of the page. Reasons to report a group include spam; scams; hate speech; attacks on individual group members; mention of violence, crime, or self-harm; or nudity, pornography, or sexually explicit content.

Creating Facebook Groups

With Facebook Groups, it's simple to set up and start using a group. You can create a Facebook group to

- Discuss a hobby or special interest with other like-minded people
- Share news and information with members of a specific professional organization
- Privately communicate with colleagues, clients, or family members
- Create a public community related to your business

The main "rule" that Facebook has concerning groups is that you can't create a racist, sexist, or hate group. A reasonable discussion or debate about current events or a hot topic is fine, as long as your group doesn't cross the line. If you create a group that violates Facebook's rules, your group will be deleted and your Facebook account could be terminated.

SHOW ME   Media 10.4—Creating Your Own Group
*Access this video file through your registered Web Edition at
my.safaribooksonline.com/9780132117029/media.*

LET ME TRY IT

Create Your Own Group

To create your own group on Facebook, follow these steps:

1. From your Facebook home page, click the Create Group link in the left column. The Create Group dialog box opens (see Figure 10.13).

Figure 10.13   *Set up your new group in the Create Group dialog box.*

2. In the Group Name field, enter a name that clearly identifies your group. If you want other Facebook members to find your group in search results, be sure to use keywords related to your group's topic.

3. If you already know the names of Facebook friends who will be members of this group, enter their names in the Members text box. As you type, Facebook displays a list of your friends whose names match what you've typed so far.

Only add group members who are aware you're adding them to your group. Otherwise, you should wait until after you've created your group to invite friends to join. For example, if a group of colleagues, friends, or family members mutually agree to participate in a Facebook group, go ahead and enter these people in the Members text box. If your friends aren't aware of your new group, it's proper Facebook etiquette to invite them to join rather than add them by default.

4. Select the Privacy level for your group from the drop-down list. Options include open, closed, and secret groups. See "Understanding How Groups Work" earlier in this chapter for more information about these group types.

5. Click the Create button to create your group. Facebook displays your new group (see Figure 10.14).

Figure 10.14 *Your new group awaits content and participation.*

If you added people to your group, Facebook notifies you of this in a dialog box. Click the Okay button to close this dialog box.

From here, you should set up a group email address, add a profile picture, and specify who has admin rights to manage your group.

Administering Your Group

As the creator of a group you have certain rights that regular group members don't have. For example, you can set up a group email address, add a profile picture, give admin rights to other group members, and choose whether or not to accept new group members.

 SHOW ME   Media 10.5—Administering Your Group
Access this video file through your registered Web Edition at
my.safaribooksonline.com/9780132117029/media.

Setting Up a Group Email Address

Setting up a group email address enables you to quickly stay in touch with group members outside of Facebook.

 LET ME TRY IT

Set Up a Group Email Address

To set up a group email address, follow these steps:

1. On your group page (refer to Figure 10.14), click the Edit Group button in the upper-right corner. The Basic Information page opens, shown in Figure 10.15.

2. Optionally, edit the group name or privacy settings you specified when you set up your group.

3. Click the Set Up Group Email button to open the Create Group Email Address dialog box, shown in Figure 10.16.

4. Enter an email address for your group. All group email addresses end with the suffix @groups.facebook.com. When anyone sends an email to the address you enter, everyone in the group receives it.

5. Click the Create Email button. Facebook replaces the Set Up Group Email button with a link to your group's email address, which you can't change.

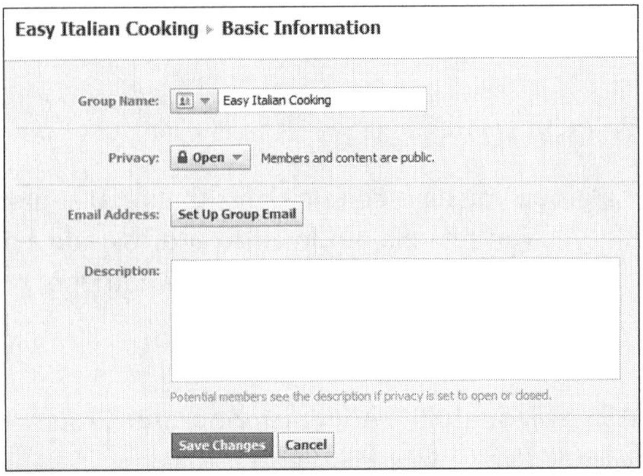

Figure 10.15   *Edit basic information about your new group.*

Figure 10.16   *Contact group members directly via email.*

If the email address you want is already taken, Facebook asks you to choose another name.

6. Enter a description of your group in the Description text box. Using target keywords in your description is particularly important if you want to attract new members to your group.

7. Click the Save Changes button.

To send an email message to your group, click the link in the Email Address. Your default email client opens where you can write and send your message.

Personalizing Your Group with a Picture

Placing a picture or logo in the upper-left corner of your group page helps to personalize your group. Facebook also uses a thumbnail of this picture on other parts of the site, such as in group search results.

 LET ME TRY IT

Insert a Group Picture

To add a picture or logo to the upper-left corner of your group's page, follow these steps:

1. Click the Edit Group button in the upper-right corner of your group's page.

2. Click the Profile Picture tab on the left side of the page.

3. Choose one of the following options on the Profile Picture page (see Figure 10.17).

Figure 10.17   *Upload a picture or take one with your webcam.*

- **Browse**—Select and upload a picture from your computer.
- **Take a Picture**—Use your webcam to take and insert a picture.

Your picture now displays in the upper-left corner of your group, as shown in Figure 10.18. Click the Edit Thumbnail link below this picture on the Profile Picture page to edit your group's thumbnail picture. To remove a picture, click the Remove Your Picture link.

Edit Thumbnail
Remove Your Picture

Figure 10.18   *Personalize your group with a relevant picture or logo.*

Assigning Group Administrators

As a group creator, Facebook assigns you administrator (admin) rights automatically. You can also give other group members admin rights if you want to share this responsibility. An admin can perform the following tasks, unavailable to regular group members:

- Send group messages
- Edit group settings
- Change a group's picture
- Assign admin and officer rights to other members
- Remove members
- Revoke the admin rights of admins who have shorter tenure than they do

 LET ME TRY IT

Make a Group Member an Admin

To make someone a group admin, follow these steps:

1. Click the Edit Group button on the right side of your group.

2. Click the Members tab on the left side of the page.

3. Click the Make Admin link below the name of the member you want to assign this designation to, as shown in Figure 10.19.

Figure 10.19   *You can make any of your existing group members an admin.*

4. In the Make [Person's Name] a Group Admin dialog box, click the Make Admin button to confirm this task.

To remove a member's admin rights, click the Remove Admin link below this person's name on the Members tab. Remember that you can revoke only the rights of someone who has less group tenure than you do.

As a group creator, Facebook assigns you administrator (admin) rights automatically. You can also give other group members admin rights if you want to share this responsibility. An admin can perform the following tasks, unavailable to regular group members: Send group messages, edit group settings, change a group's picture, assign admin rights to other members, remove members, and revoke the admin rights of admins who have shorter tenure than they do.

Approving Group Members

When someone requests to join your group, Facebook notifies you via the red alert Notifications icon in the upper-left corner of the screen. Requests to join a group also appear on the group page itself—if you're a group admin.

 LET ME TRY IT

Approve a Request to Join Your Group

To approve someone as a group member, follow these steps:

1. On your group page, review open requests in the Requests section in the right column (see Figure 10.20).

Figure 10.20 *Quickly approve or ignore group member requests.*

2. Click the Add button to the right of the people you want to accept into your group. The people you approve move to the Members list.

3. Click the Ignore button to the right of the people you don't want to accept into your group.

4. If you have many requests, click the See All link to view and respond to your complete list of requests.

Removing Group Members

Group admins have the right to remove or even ban group members. If a person is leaving a group on good terms, a removal is all that's required. If someone is disrupting your group or posting content that violates Facebook's terms and conditions, you can remove *and* ban this person. Banned members can't find the group in search results and can no longer see any group contents. If you choose not to ban group members you remove, they can request to rejoin your group again.

 LET ME TRY IT

Remove a Group Member

To remove a group member, follow these steps:

1. Click the Edit Group button on the right side of your group page.

2. Click the Members tab on the left side of the group page.

3. Click the Remove (x) button to the right of the member you want to remove. Figure 10.21 shows the Remove dialog box, which opens.

4. Optionally, click the Ban Permanently checkbox.

5. Click the Confirm button to confirm the removal.

Figure 10.21   *Admins can remove or ban other group members.*

Deleting Your Group

If you decide that you no longer want to maintain your group, you can delete it. To do so, delete all group members and then click the Leave Group link at the bottom of the left sidebar to delete yourself.

This chapter describes how events work, how to
find existing events, and how to create your
own events.

11

Joining and Creating Events

Facebook makes it easy for you to work with events on the site. You can search for
events to attend, view the events you've attended and those your friends are planning to attend, and create your own events, including those that include others
and those meant to promote awareness, such as a pet safety day.

In this chapter, you explore the many ways to manage events. You'll understand
different ways to locate an event, how public and private events work, and how to
communicate changes about your event. You can even invite people who do not
use Facebook to your event. You can also listen to tips and watch videos that show
you step-by-step how to make event management easy.

How Events Work

Facebook's event application is easy to use and powerful. You can use it to organize
simple get-togethers or major events in a snap. You, as the event *admin*, create the
event and manage the guest list. You also have all of Facebook's tools, such as wall
posts and Feed stories, to keep your guests informed about the latest updates.

Facebook provides two types of events based on privacy:

- **Public event**—Gatherings such as a concert or fair are examples of a public
  event. Everyone can see the event in event search and put himself on the
  guest list. Also, anyone attending can invite friends to the event. Finally,
  updates such as wall posts and photos are also viewable by everyone.

- **Private event**—Use a private event to keep a surprise party or event a secret.
  This type of event does not show up in search or in your profile. The event
  admin must invite guests to attend. Finally, only invited guests can see the
  event in their News Feed.

If your event was created before Facebook's shift to Public and Private event types, it should maintain its previous settings. New events will always use the two new event categories.

Only Facebook members can view Facebook-created events. Although you can notify your friends via email about an event, they need to log in to Facebook to view event details.

Be aware of the risk when meeting new people in person! You don't have the online safeguards such as block lists to protect you if something unexpected happens. You can minimize your online risks by reading Chapter 6, "Safeguarding Your Information on Facebook." However, when venturing into the real world, be aware some people may behave differently in real life than they do online.

 TELL ME MORE　　**Media 11.1—How Events Work**

Access this audio recording through your registered Web Edition at **my.safaribooksonline.com/9780132117029/media.**

Searching for an Event

You can find events in three ways. By searching events using keywords, you can pick from all events posted on Facebook. Another approach is to view events your friends are hosting or planning to attend. The third approach is to look at your previously attended events.

- **Find events using keywords**—You can search on keywords, such as "hiking," by using Facebook's search box. Results can be filtered by date and event type.

- **View your friends' events**—Viewing your friends' events, whether they are hosting one or planning to attend, is a good way to find an event that you'll like.

- **Look at your past events**—You can review a list of events you've created and attended to see if any are worth repeating.

If the steps in the following sections don't match what you see online, check out this book's online media. The online media is revised whenever Facebook rolls out a major update.

Searching for an Event using Facebook's Search

One of the fastest ways to locate an event is to search for it through Facebook search. You will need to use one or more keywords that describe the event you're looking for. Keep in mind the results from search can be very broad.

 SHOW ME   Media 11.2—Searching for Events Using Facebook's Search
Access this video file through your registered Web Edition at
my.safaribooksonline.com/9780132117029/media.

 LET ME TRY IT

Search for Events Using Facebook's Search

To search for events using Facebook's search, follow these steps:

1.   Select Home at the top of the page (see Figure 11.1).

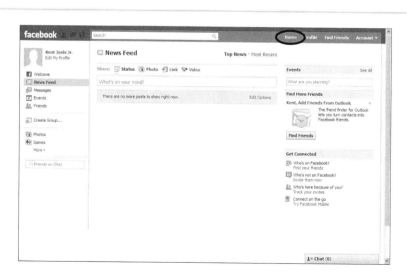

Figure 11.1   *Use Facebook's Home button to navigate to your Home page.*

2. Select the search box and type one or more words about the event. Click the magnifying glass icon (see Figure 11.2).

Figure 11.2   *Use Facebook's generic search box to search for an event.*

3. Select **Events** to just show events (see Figure 11.3).

Figure 11.3   *Select Events to see only events.*

4. Select an event to see more details (see Figure 11.4).

Figure 11.4   *An Event page with time, location, and one attendee.*

Searching Your Friends' Events to Find an Event

You can also search on your friends' events. You can see events that they are planning to attend or are hosting. The assumption is that you'll probably be interested in the same types of events, so the results from this search may be more tailored to your interests than a generic one. Obviously, you need to be connected to at least one friend to search on friend's events.

 SHOW ME Media 11.3—Searching for Events Your Friends Are Attending or Hosting

Access this video file through your registered Web Edition at
my.safaribooksonline.com/9780132117029/media.

 LET ME TRY IT

Search for Events Your Friends Are Attending or Hosting

To search for events your friends are attending or hosting, follow these steps:

1. Select Home at the top of your page.

2. Select Events under your profile picture to just show events (see Figure 11.5).

Figure 11.5 *Select Events to see your events.*

3. Select Friends' Events within that menu.

4. You see a list of your friends' upcoming events.

If you see a long list of events for a friend, select Older Posts to see all of his events. You can find this option at the bottom of his event list.

Reviewing Your Past Events

Your past events are the narrowest but most tailored way to search for events. Perhaps you want to rehost an event or you'd like to attend the same event again. You can scan through your event history to refresh your memory of events you attended or were planning to attend.

 LET ME TRY IT

Review Your Past Events

To review your past events, follow these steps:

1. Select Home at the top of your page.

2. Select Events under your profile picture to just show events.

3. Select Past Events and you'll see a list of past events you've hosted or attended (see Figure 11.6).

Figure 11.6 *Select Past Events to see your previous events.*

At the bottom of the page (refer to Figure 11.6), Export Events lets you save events to your favorite calendar program such as Microsoft Outlook, Google Calendar, or Apple iCal.

Participating in an Event

If you've found an event you want to attend or received an invitation, you need to let the organizer know whether you are attending. You do this based on how you know about the event:

- **You received an invite**—Facebook provides a RSVP page to communicate your choice to attend or not and to add a note with your response. Remember, you receive an invite for both public and private events.

- **You know about the event, but didn't get an invite**—Perhaps you found the event through Facebook's search or saw an event your friend was planning to attend. If the event is public, you can invite yourself using Facebook's RSVP box. If the event is private but you still want to attend, you can try asking for an invite. Contact the organizer listed on the event's or event admin's page.

RSVPing to an Invitation

You've received the invite, now you need to reply with your plans. Facebook's RSVP box lets you indicate your choice to attend, maybe attend, or not attend. You can also send an optional note to the host.

 SHOW ME   Media 11.4—RSVPing When You've Received a Personal Invitation

Access this video file through your registered Web Edition at my.safaribooksonline.com/9780132117029/media.

 LET ME TRY IT

RSVP When You Receive a Personal Invitation

To RSVP when you receive a personal invitation, follow these steps:

1. Select Home at the top of your page.

2. Select Events under your profile picture.

3. Select Respond next to the event (see Figure 11.7).

Figure 11.7   *An event you've been invited to.*

4. Select your choice from Attending, Maybe Attending, or Not Attending. If you want, you can add an optional note (see Figure 11.8).

Figure 11.8   *RSVP choices for an event.*

5. Select RSVP to send your note (refer to Figure 11.8).

RSVPing to a Public Event without an Invitation

If you've found an event your friend is attending or through Facebook search, it's still beneficial to let the organizer know you are attending their event. Just like RSVPing when you receive an invitation, you use Facebook's RSVP box to indicate your choice to attend, maybe attend, or not attend. You can also send an optional note to the host.

LET ME TRY IT

RSVP to a Public Event without an Invitation

To RSVP to a public event without an invitation, follow these steps:

1. Select RSVP next to the event (see Figure 11.9).

Figure 11.9   *A public event you want to attend.*

2. Select your choice of Attending, Maybe Attending, or Not Attending. If you want, you can add an optional note (refer to Figure 11.8).

3. Select RSVP to send your note (refer to Figure 11.8).

Creating Your Own Event

Facebook makes it simple to create an event. You only need four pieces of information: what's planned, when it is, where it is located, and who's invited. With this in hand, you can spread the word about any event whether it's a simple lunch to a grand opening or a global "attend in spirit" event. When your friends RSVP to your event, their friends will notice and may consider attending. Facebook does a great job of increasing your event's popularity through friends.

Creating an Event with Basic Information

After you've created your event, you can add to its basic information. All these options are not required but do build an event posting that's informative and interesting:

- **Who's invited**—An event created for one person can be peaceful or lonely depending on your perspective. If you're interested in inviting some friends, the event application lets you notify your guests on Facebook. You can also invite people who haven't joined Facebook by using their email addresses. You can't invite people who are not your Facebook friends until one of you accepts a friend request.

- **Where is it**—You can add a detailed street address, which makes your event easier to find. At the same time, you lose a little privacy. Uninvited guests could theoretically find your event and show up.

- **Privacy**—By default, the event application assumes you want a public event allowing everyone on Facebook to view it and RSVP. If that matches the event you're planning, such as a convention, then you're all set. If not, you need to change this setting. Another event setting controls whether attendees can view your guest list.

- **Event Photo**—You can add a photo or logo to draw attention to your event.

 SHOW ME Media 11.5—Creating an Event with Basic Information
Access this video file through your registered Web Edition at
my.safaribooksonline.com/9780132117029/media.

 LET ME TRY IT

Create an Event with Basic Information

To create an event with basic information, follow these steps:

1. Select Home at the top of your page.

2. Type a description in the What are you planning? field (see Figure 11.10).

Figure 11.10 *Use these fields to describe your event.*

3. Select a day and time (see Figure 11.10).

4. Type in the event location in the Where? field (see Figure 11.10).

5. Invite attendees by typing their name in Who's invited? (see Figure 11.10).

6. If you want, select Add Details to add information such as event end time, street address, and photo. You can also change the event's privacy options, which control who can RSVP and whether the guest list is presented on the event page (see Figure 11.11).

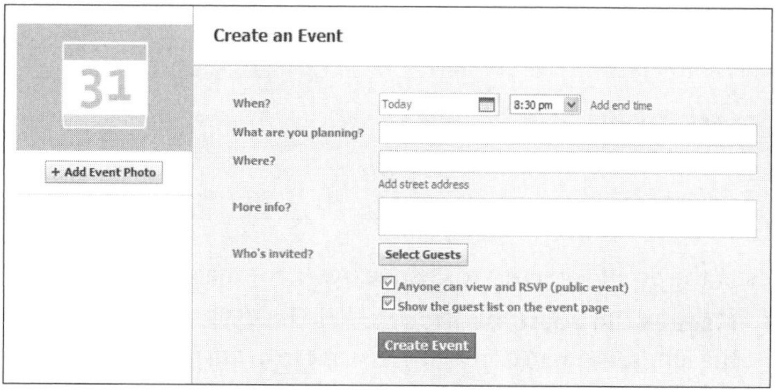

Figure 11.11   *Add or change additional event details using this window.*

If you don't see the form in Figure 11.11, select Home, Events, and the + Create an Event button at the top of the page.

7. Select Create Event to finish (refer Figure 11.11).

Viewing and Changing Your Event

Facebook provides several ways to view and manage events. You can always see your past and upcoming events plus your friends' events. With event admin permissions, you can also edit events, invite more guests, and send a message to everyone invited.

To see your events, your friends' events, or their birthdays, select Events under your profile picture from your Home page. Then select the event type you're interested in (refer to Figure 11.5).

Changing an Event

As the event host, sometimes your plans change. You may need to update the time, location, or guest list of your event based on these changes. Sometimes, you need to spruce up an event with a photo or send a message to certain guests, for example those who replied Maybe, reminding them to confirm by a certain day. We cover doing all of this in the following section.

SHOW ME Media 11.6—Changing an Event
Access this video file through your registered Web Edition at my.safaribooksonline.com/9780132117029/media.

LET ME TRY IT

Changing an Event

1. Select the event you want to change. You have these basic options:

   - **Manage the guest list**—You can see the RSVP status of your guests on the left (see Figure 11.12). If you want to invite more guests, choose Select Guests to Invite. The window to invite friends that appears is the same one you previously used when creating your event. If you need to refresh your memory and see how to work with this window, see the previous section "Creating an Event with Basic Information."

Figure 11.12 *Choose one or more of these basic options to change your event.*

   - **Broadcast to your guest list**—To send a message to all invited guests, regardless of whether they plan to attend, type your message in the Write Something... box in the middle of the screen and select Share (see Figure 11.12). Even guests who have declined to attend your event see your post.

2. Select Edit Event, in the upper right, to change additional details or to cancel your event.

3. Change your event using one or more of these settings (see Figure 11.13):

Figure 11.13   *Use this window to change your event or cancel it.*

- **Event photo**—Select Add Event Photo to add a photo or logo to draw attention to your event.

- **Add a street address**—As mentioned earlier, providing this makes your event easier to find, but you lose some privacy. Uninvited guests could theoretically show up to the get-together. Select Add Street Address to provide an address.

- **Privacy**—By default, the event application assumes you want a public event allowing everyone on Facebook to view it and RSVP. If that matches the event you're planning, such as a convention, then you're all set. If not, you need to uncheck Anyone Can View and RSVP (Public Event). If you don't want to display the guest list on the event page, uncheck Show the Guest List on the Event Page.

- **Cancel event**—This cannot be undone. Select Cancel This Event to open a new window (see Figure 11.14). You can send an optional note with your cancellation to everyone invited. Cancelled events do not show under Past Events. Select Yes, I'm Sure to complete the cancellation.

4. Select Back to Event, in the upper right, to return to the basic event page (refer to Figure 11.13).

5. Select Message Guests to communicate based on attendee RSVP response of All, Attending, Maybe Attending, or Not Yet Replied (see Figure 11.15).

6. Choose the audience you want to message based on their RSVP response from the Attendee menu (see Figure 11.16).

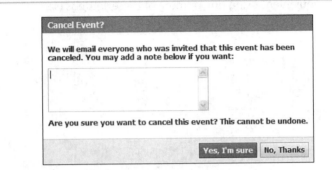

Figure 11.14   *Use this window to cancel your event and add an optional note.*

Figure 11.15   *Select Message Guests for a window to communicate with your guests.*

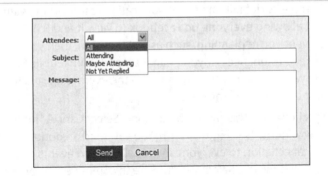

Figure 11.16   *Select how a guest RSVPed to your event.*

7. Type your subject and message and select Send to send the message (see Figure 11.17).

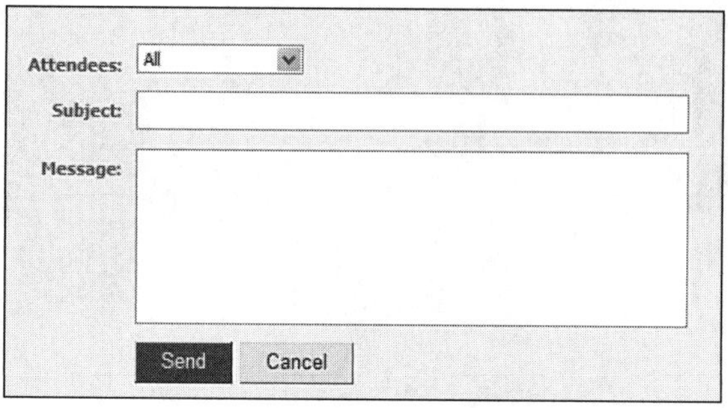

Figure 11.17   *Select Send to send a message to your guests.*

This chapter explores buying and selling using the
Facebook Marketplace application.

12

Buying and Selling with Facebook Marketplace

Millions of Facebook members use the Marketplace application to buy and sell products and services. It's an easy, free online classifieds solution for anyone wanting to do business within their Facebook network.

In this chapter, you explore the many features of Facebook Marketplace. You can also watch videos that show you how to access Facebook Marketplace, post a Marketplace listing, and manage your listings.

Understanding Facebook Marketplace

Facebook created the Marketplace application through its partnership with the online classifieds site Oodle. With Marketplace, you can post and respond to classified listings for a variety of products and services, all within the familiar Facebook environment.

There are no fees for individuals to use Marketplace to buy or sell. If you run a business and want to post numerous ads, however, consider upgrading to Oodle Pro (http://apps.facebook.com/marketplace/pro/) for more advanced features and options.

Marketplace listings fall into the following categories:

- Stuff
- Vehicle
- Rentals
- Real Estate
- Jobs
- Tickets
- Services
- Community
- Pets

Although there's a long list of what you can buy and sell on Marketplace, some items are prohibited. For a list of prohibited content, scroll down to the bottom of the Marketplace page and click the Prohibited Content link. Some examples of prohibited content include alcoholic beverages, tobacco, weapons, stocks and securities, hazardous materials, prescription drugs, pesticides, and fireworks. The list also includes some things most reasonable users wouldn't consider selling anyway such as body parts, stolen property, counterfeit products, and items for use in committing a crime.

Accessing Facebook Marketplace

Depending on your past Facebook activity, a link to Marketplace might already exist on Facebook's left sidebar (see Figure 12.1). If you have a lot of bookmarks, click the More link to expand your list.

Figure 12.1   *Get easy access to Marketplace from Facebook's left sidebar.*

If the Marketplace link is there, click it to open the Marketplace application, shown in Figure 12.2.

SHOW ME   Media 12.1—Accessing Facebook Marketplace
Access this video file through your registered Web Edition at
my.safaribooksonline.com/9780132117029/media.

If no Marketplace link exists, you can add the application and create a sidebar bookmark to it for easy access.

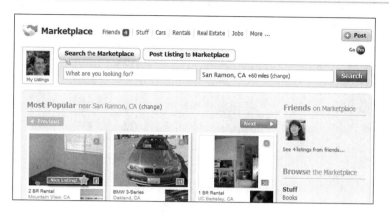

Figure 12.2 *Marketplace lets you buy and sell within your Facebook network.*

 LET ME TRY IT

Add Marketplace

To add the Marketplace application and bookmark it, follow these steps:

1. Enter **Marketplace** in the search box at the top of the Facebook screen and click the Search button.

2. Select Marketplace App from the drop-down menu that opens.

3. On the Marketplace page (see Figure 12.3), click the Go to App button.

Figure 12.3 *Learn more about Marketplace or go directly to the app.*

4. On Marketplace, click the Connect with Friends button, as shown in Figure 12.4.

Figure 12.4 *Connect with your friends on Marketplace to view their listings.*

5. On the Request for Permission page (see Figure 12.5), click the Allow button to give Marketplace access to your Facebook profile data.

Figure 12.5 *Give Facebook permission to connect with your friends on Marketplace.*

Facebook enables you to view your friends' listings on Marketplace and adds a bookmark to the left column of your home page.

Shopping on Marketplace

Shopping on Marketplace is easy. In just a few minutes, you can browse your friends' listings or search for a specific item you want.

On the Marketplace page (refer to Figure 12.2), click the See [Number] Listings from Friends link to view listings posted by your friends, friends of friends, and people in shared networks.

If this page displays too many results, you can narrow results in the Posted By and Category boxes (see Figure 12.6).

Figure 12.6 *Buy and sell within your Facebook network of friends.*

Searching Marketplace

If you want to find something specific on Marketplace, you can click one of the category links in the Browse the Marketplace section. Or, you can search for specific keywords.

 LET ME TRY IT

Search Marketplace Listings

To search Marketplace listings, follow these steps:

1. Go to the Marketplace application page on Facebook. You can access it directly at http://apps.facebook.com/marketplace/ or click the Marketplace link on Facebook's left sidebar.

2. Click a category link in the Browse the Marketplace list, shown in Figure 12.7. For more information about these categories, see "Understanding Facebook Marketplace" earlier in this chapter.

Figure 12.7   *Search for Marketplace items in a variety of categories.*

3. Facebook displays search results. If you don't find what you're looking for in these search results, you can narrow your search by:

   - Entering keywords in the Search for text box at the top of the page and clicking the Search button.
   - Click the Change link to the right of your location to change location and radius information. Click the Search button when you're finished.
   - Click one of the search filters on the left side of the page (see Figure 12.8). These vary based on the type of item you're searching for.

4. To view a specific listing, click its title. If the Links to Partner button displays in the listing box, Facebook takes you to an external website to view the ad. Otherwise, you view an ad placed by an individual Facebook user.

Responding to a Marketplace Listing

If you click a Marketplace listing that includes the Links to Partner button, you need to follow the instructions on the external site. If you click a Marketplace listing posted by an individual Facebook member, you view the listing on Facebook. Figure 12.9 shows a sample listing.

Figure 12.8 *Narrow your search results to find exactly what you're looking for.*

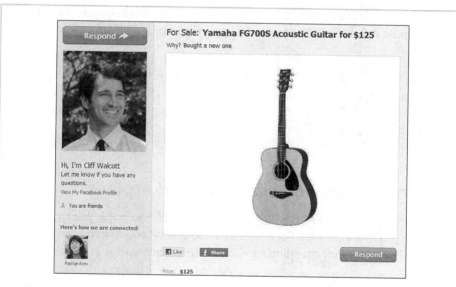

Figure 12.9 *Open a listing to view its details.*

On a Facebook listing, you can

- Click the Respond button to open the New Message dialog box, shown in Figure 12.10, where you can enter a message to the poster.

- Add a comment to the listing for public view.

- Click the Like button to let others know you like this listing.

Figure 12.10 *Respond to the person who posted a Marketplace listing.*

- Click the Share button to share a post about this listing on your profile.

- Report this listing to Facebook by clicking the Tools link. In general, you should only report listings you feel are inappropriate, illegal, or fraudulent.

Remember to stay safe when using Facebook Marketplace. Although most listings are legitimate efforts to sell something, be wary of any listings that seem suspicious. Also, use caution when revealing any personal information such as your address or phone number.

Posting Listings on Facebook Marketplace

If you have something to sell and want to market it on Facebook, you can post a listing in just a few minutes. For a reminder about what you can and can't sell on Marketplace, see "Understanding Facebook Marketplace" earlier in this chapter.

SHOW ME   Media 12.2—Posting a Listing on Facebook Marketplace
Access this video file through your registered Web Edition at
my.safaribooksonline.com/9780132117029/media.

 **LET ME TRY IT**

Post a Listing on Facebook Marketplace

To list something on Marketplace, follow these steps:

1. Go to the Marketplace application page on Facebook. You can access it directly at http://apps.facebook.com/marketplace/ or click the Marketplace link on Facebook's left sidebar.

2. On the Marketplace page, click the Post button (refer to Figure 12.2).

> You can also post a listing by clicking the Post Listing to Marketplace button.

3. In the Post a Listing dialog box (see Figure 12.11), select a category from the drop-down list. Your choices include: Stuff, Vehicle, Rentals, Houses, Jobs, Services, Tickets, Pets, or Community.

Figure 12.11   *Select the best category for what you want to sell.*

4. The Post a Listing dialog box displays additional fields related to your selection in Step 3. Figure 12.12 shows an example of the fields that display if you select the Stuff category.

5. Click the Continue button to open an expanded version of the Post a Listing dialog box, customized to your choices in Steps 3 and 4 (see Figure 12.13).

6. Enter additional details in the expanded Post a Listing dialog box, such a listing heading, price, photo, and more. The information you post varies based on what you're selling.

7. When you finish entering your listing details, click the Post button.

Figure 12.12 *Additional fields display when you select your category.*

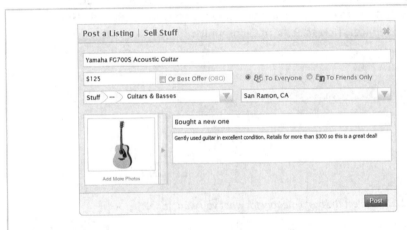

Figure 12.13 *Enter details about what you want to sell.*

8. In the Request for Permission dialog box (see Figure 12.14), click the Allow button to allow Facebook to email you directly about your listing and to post your listing to your Wall.

9. Facebook notifies you that your listing is in progress (see Figure 12.15), which can take up to 30 minutes to process and become live.

If you're new to Marketplace, Facebook sends you an email to verify your listing. Click the link in this email to confirm and publish.

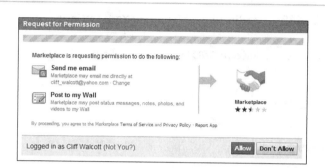

Figure 12.14 *Give Facebook permission to contact you about your listing.*

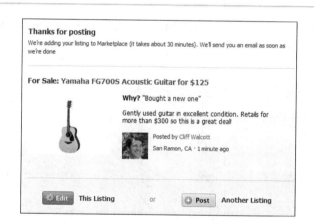

Figure 12.15 *Within 30 minutes, your Marketplace listing should be live on Facebook.*

Your listing displays on Marketplace for 30 days.

When other Facebook users respond to your listing, you receive an email notification. For more information about how the buying process works, see "Shopping on Marketplace" earlier in this chapter. You must negotiate purchasing and delivery options individually with any buyer.

Editing Your Listings

If you need to change an active listing, you can easily edit it. For example, you might discover a typo, want to change a category, or remove or replace a photo.

SHOW ME   Media 12.3—Managing Your Listings
Access this video file through your registered Web Edition at
my.safaribooksonline.com/9780132117029/media.

LET ME TRY IT

Edit an Active Listing

To edit an active Marketplace listing, follow these steps:

1. Go to the Marketplace application page on Facebook. You can access it directly at http://apps.facebook.com/marketplace/ or click the Marketplace link on Facebook's left sidebar.

2. On the Marketplace page, click the My Listings link below your photo (see Figure 12.16).

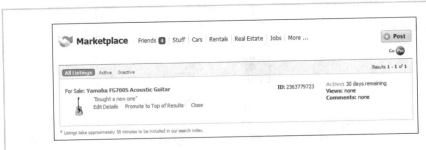

Figure 12.16   *You can easily manage your Marketplace listings.*

3. Below the listing you want to promote, click the Edit Details link. The Edit Your Listing dialog box opens as shown in Figure 12.17.

To delete an attached photo, pause your mouse over the thumbnail and click the Delete (x) button.

4. Make your changes and click the Post button to update your listing, which can take up to 30 minutes to process.

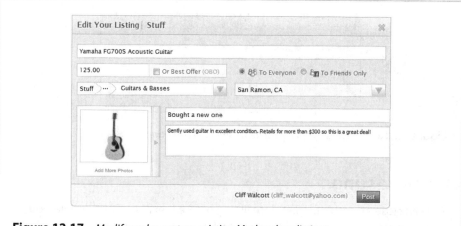

Figure 12.17   *Modify and repost an existing Marketplace listing.*

Promoting Listings to the Top of Results

If you aren't getting the results you want from your Marketplace listing, consider doing some promotion. Facebook allows you to republish your listings once every 24 hours. Doing so republishes it to your Facebook wall and moves it to the top of the Marketplace search results.

 LET ME TRY IT

Promote a Listing to the Top of Results

To promote your listing to the top of results, follow these steps:

1. Go to the Marketplace application page on Facebook. You can access it directly at http://apps.facebook.com/marketplace/ or click the Marketplace link on Facebook's left sidebar.

2. On the Marketplace page, click the My Listings link below your photo.

3. Below the listing you want to promote, click the Promote to Top of Results link.

4. In the Promote to Top of Results dialog box (see Figure 12.18), click the Okay button to confirm that you want to promote your listing.

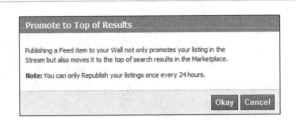

Figure 12.18   *Republish your listing for additional promotion.*

Closing Listings

You can close an active Marketplace listing before it expires. For example, you might sell your item or decide that you no longer want to sell it.

 LET ME TRY IT

Close a Listing

To close a Marketplace listing, follow these steps:

1. Go to the Marketplace application page on Facebook. You can access it directly at http://apps.facebook.com/marketplace/ or click the Market-place link on Facebook's left sidebar.

2. On the Marketplace application page, click the My Listings link below your photo.

3. Below the listing you want to close, click the Close link.

4. In the Close Listing dialog box (see Figure 12.19), click the Yes option button to confirm that you want to close.

5. Click the Close Listing button.

Figure 12.19   *Close a listing if your item sells.*

Facebook closes your listing. It's no longer active on Marketplace, but remains on your Inactive tab.

You can't completely delete a Marketplace listing, just close it.

Reposting Expired Listings

Your Marketplace listings expire in 30 days, whether or not you sell anything. Facebook notifies you of the listing expiration with an email, which contains a link for reposting your listing.

Alternatively, you can repost in the Marketplace app itself.

 LET ME TRY IT

Repost an Expired Listing

To repost a Marketplace listing, follow these steps:

1. Go to the Marketplace application page on Facebook. You can access it directly at http://apps.facebook.com/marketplace/ or click the Marketplace link on Facebook's left sidebar.

2. On the Marketplace applications page, click the My Listings link below your photo.

3. Click the title of the listing you want to repost.

4. Click the Repost button on this page. Note that this button displays only if your listing is available to repost.

Facebook reposts your listing for another 30 days with a new ID number.

You can repost a listing only one time. After that, you need to create a new listing if you want to list the same item again.

Removing the Marketplace Application

If you no longer want to use Marketplace, you can remove it.

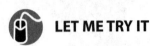 **LET ME TRY IT**

Remove Marketplace

To remove the Marketplace app, follow these steps:

1. Select Privacy Settings from the Account drop-down menu.

2. Scroll down to the bottom of the Choose Your Privacy Settings page and click the Edit Your Settings link.

3. Click the Edit Settings button to the right of the Apps You Use section.

4. On the Apps, Games, and Websites page, click the X button (Remove) to the right of the Marketplace listing, as shown in Figure 12.20.

Figure 12.20   *Remove the Marketplace app if you no longer want to use it.*

5. In the Remove Marketplace? dialog box, click the Remove button to confirm that you want to remove this application.

Be aware that removing Marketplace means that you no longer have access to this application and your listings, although you can add the application again at any time in the future. Facebook also removes the Marketplace bookmark and the My Listings tab. Removing Marketplace, however, doesn't delete any Marketplace listings you created.

This chapter explores how to find applications and change your Facebook experience through using applications.

13

Using Facebook Applications

Although you might not notice it, you already use Facebook applications. When you upload a video, you use the Video application. When you create an event, you use yet another application. Facebook has developed a set of built-in applications that we, as Facebook users, take for granted, such as Video, Photos, and Groups, to name a few.

People who create applications are constantly developing, improving, and publishing Facebook applications. Their purposes range from serious and utility based to light-hearted entertainment such as the Pillow Fight application. You can browse through these and other applications on the Application Directory page as described in another section.

Although there are currently several hundred thousand active applications on Facebook, they all have a standard set of features at the time of this writing which is in early 2011. They all have pages so you can get more information, read and post reviews, and contact the developer. You must grant permission to any application before it interacts with your Facebook account. You can see and restrict the information the application uses and may share with your friends. This is described in more detail in Chapter 6, "Safeguarding Your Information on Facebook." Finally, you can block or completely remove any unwanted applications or those that have become 'spammy.'

If you are interested in creating Facebook applications, see http://developers. facebook.com.

 TELL ME MORE   Media 13.1—Using Facebook Applications
Access this audio recording through your registered Web Edition at
my.safaribooksonline.com/9780132117029/media.

Finding an Application

There are several ways to find an application. Here are three ways:

- **Search for it**—You can look for an application in Facebook Search at the top of every page. This is probably the fastest way if you know the application name and how to use Facebook Search.

- **Through your friends**—You might get an application request from a friend who's already using it or see it in use on their profile or News Feed. For example, if your friend has joined a nonprofit cause, they may send you an invite to use the Causes applications to see if you're joining the cause with them.

- **Browse the Application Directory**—You can also find all active and experimental applications on Facebook on the Application Directory page. Facebook uses filters to locate applications similar to filtering on News Feed. Applications are filtered or organized into categories based on use such as Just for Fun.

Responding to a Friend's Application Request

When your friends use an application they want to share with you or have you participate with them in, you get an application request. Although there are several ways an application presents the request, the basic choices are for you to accept, find out more about the application, or hide the request from your profile.

You'll find applications requests by selecting App Requests under your profile picture on your profile page. If you want to learn more about the application before making a response, visit the application's page. You do this by clicking on the application's name (see Figure 13.1). An application's page is described in more detail later in the chapter.

If you've made a decision about the request, you can agree to install the application by selecting Accept or hide the request by selecting 'X' (see Figure 13.1).

If you get spammed with application invites from a friend, you can block their requests. You can find this choice under Account, Privacy Settings, Edit Your Lists (under Block Lists). To read more about this, see Chapter 6.

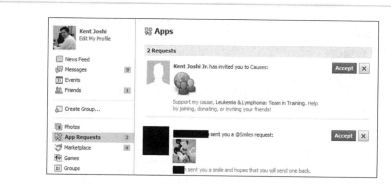

Figure 13.1   *Use application requests from friends as another way to find applications.*

Navigating the Application Directory

The Application Directory holds every application on Facebook no matter if they are large or small, new or old, experimental or fully tested. You can find the Application Directory by typing www.facebook.com/apps. This may seem like extra typing, but Facebook may add a more direct path in the future.

The Application Directory has two areas. Application categories are on the left side of the page and applications choices are in the middle of the page. There is also a drop-down menu in the middle of the page to further narrow a category down. For example, the drop-menu for Friends and Family has Friends, Family, Pets, and Other. Some of the main categories may need an explanation (see Figure 13.2):

- **All Applications**—This category displays all applications in all categories.

- **On Facebook**—This category is for applications run solely on the Facebook Platform or the application toolkit Facebook provides to developers to make applications.

- **External Websites**—This category contains applications that are connected with an external website.

- **Mobile**—These applications are focused on mobility solutions and are part of Facebook, but they have a mobile component connected to mobile devices such as the Blackberry or iPhone.

- **Desktop**—Similar to the Mobile category, these are Desktop applications.

Figure 13.2   *Browse the Application Directory as another way to find an application.*

- **Prototypes**—This category holds all the experimental applications developed by Facebook engineers. There are no guarantees that these applications are 100% bug-free.

After you select the category you want, applications are listed in three possible sections of Featured by Facebook, Applications You May Like, and Recent Activity from Friends. This list describes these sections in more detail (see Figure 13.3):

- **Featured by Facebook**—This section lists the applications that the Facebook team periodically selects. Use the two triangles to scroll through the pages.

- **Applications You May Like**—This section includes applications that are popular with your friends, based on your current favorites, or are the most popular applications on Facebook. Again, scroll through the apps using the two triangles.

- **Recent Activity from Friends**—Beneath Applications You May Like, this section contains an information stream of your friend's application activity.

 SHOW ME   Media 13.2—Navigate the Application Directory to Find an Application
Access this video file through your registered Web Edition at
my.safaribooksonline.com/9780132117029/media.

Figure 13.3   *Use the three sections of a main category to browse for an application.*

  LET ME TRY IT

Navigate the Application Directory to Find an Application

To find the popular game FarmVille using category filtering, follow these steps:

1. Type **www.facebook.com/apps** to open the Application Directory.

2. Select Games from the menu on the left (see Figure 13.4).

3. Select Virtual World from the drop-menu at the top (see Figure 13.4).

4. Select the word Popular in the middle of the page (see Figure 13.4).

5. Using your mouse, scroll until you see the game called FarmVille (see Figure 13.4). You can read the summary paragraph displayed or click on the application title to get more details or install the application.

An alternative way to find FarmVille is by typing its name in the box titled Search Apps in the top left (refer Figure 13.4).

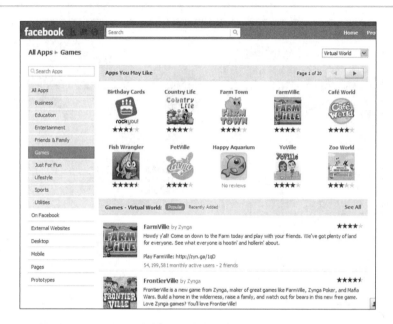

Figure 13.4 *Use category filtering to find a game.*

Working with Facebook Applications

When you find the application you want, as described in the previous section, you need to install it before you can use it. When you do, it requests permission to access information about you and your friends. This can be all right as it does this to tailor the experience of application to you. However, you want to weigh the benefits of using the application with any privacy concerns. Facebook isn't really responsible if the application misuses your personal information by accidentally exposing or selling it. You can see Chapter 6 to understand what applications share about you and how to manage that sharing. For this chapter, we're assuming the benefit of using the application outweighs any risks for you.

Sometimes you need help to use an application. It could be you want some training to do something or the application isn't doing what you expect. The more popular applications have help pages so you can troubleshoot a problem and fix it.

Sometimes you need to remove an application. If you no longer want an application, it's easy to remove it.

You can find steps to perform all of these operations in the following sections.

You can view your installed applications from the Applications Page. To get there, select Apps under your profile picture from your home page.

Installing an Application

As mentioned earlier, you need to install an application to use it. To do so, select the application title after locating it. You can follow previous sections in the chapter to locate an application. Once you are on the application's page, select Go to App (see Figure 13.5). The design of the install button may vary by application.

Figure 13.5 *Select Go to App from the application's page to begin the installation process.*

Next, select Allow if you are comfortable with the information the application needs to access to work. As you can see in the figure, some applications email you, post to your Wall, and access your list of friends (see Figure 13.6).

For most applications, you've finished the steps to install them. If there are more for your particular application, follow the given instructions until you see the application running.

 SHOW ME   Media 13.3—Installing an Application
Access this video file through your registered Web Edition at
my.safaribooksonline.com/9780132117029/media.

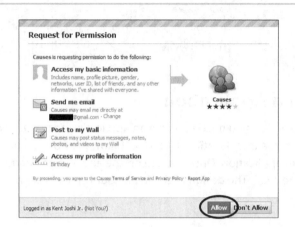

Figure 13.6 *Select Allow if you are comfortable granting permission to this application.*

Getting Help for an Application

If you have problems using an application, you have can visit its application or Help page. Sometimes, you can also find help on a website outside of Facebook. On the application's Facebook page, at a minimum, you can use its Wall to read comments and post your questions. If available, you can also use its page to contact the developer, read reviews, post in Discussions, and look at photos and videos. One way to get to the application's page is to locate the app in the Application Directory and then click on its title.

If the application has a help page, you can usually find items such as a Frequently Asked Question (FAQ) list, top issues list, and searchable list of help topics. Sometimes, a company provides a support organization so you can contact a live person. To get to an application's help page, start with the menu in the top right and select Account, Help Center, then Games and Apps from the left. Select your application from the list in the middle of the page (see Figure 13.7).

Figure 13.7 *Select an application from the Help Center to see its help page.*

Removing an Application

Sometimes, you don't want an application because you no longer need it or it has becomes spammy. When you remove an application, you also remove its access to your information, and it disappears from your bookmarks, profile, and your Application page. One of the most straightforward ways to remove it is using Facebook's Privacy page.

To get to the Privacy page, select Account (top right of any page) and then Privacy Settings. On the Privacy page, select the Edit Your Settings link in the lower left and then Remove in middle of the page (see Figure 13.8).

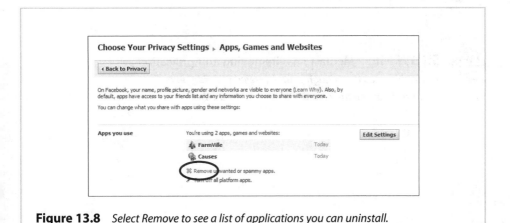

Figure 13.8 *Select Remove to see a list of applications you can uninstall.*

Then select the X to the right of the application you no longer want (see Figure 13.9)

Figure 13.9 *Select X next to the right of the application you want to uninstall.*

Select Remove from the dialog box that appears (see Figure 13.10). Finally, select OK when prompted.

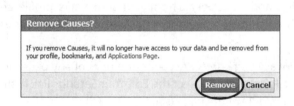

Figure 13.10   *Select Remove to uninstall the application.*

SHOW ME   Media 13.4—Removing an Application
Access this video file through your registered Web Edition at
my.safaribooksonline.com/9780132117029/media.

This chapter shows you how to grow your business or brand with a Facebook page.

14

Making Business Connections on Facebook

Facebook pages offer a great way to build community and awareness for your business or brand, within the popular framework of Facebook and its hundreds of millions of members.

In this chapter, you learn how to find, like, participate in, and create Facebook pages. You can also listen to tips on ways to use a Facebook page to build your business and watch videos that show you how to find your way around Facebook pages, create your own Facebook page, and add applications to your Facebook page.

Understanding Facebook Pages for Businesses and Brands

Facebook pages are a great tool for any business, organization, brand, or public figure (musician, athlete, author, speaker, and so forth) seeking to generate buzz and visibility as well as create a community for their supporters and fans. It's important to keep in mind, however, the difference between a Facebook page, your personal Facebook profile, and a Facebook group.

Facebook pages are often referred to as *fan pages*. This terminology comes from the time when Facebook formerly offered a Become a Fan button to encourage page visitors to show their support. This is now called the Like button.

A *Facebook page* offers a public presence for a real business, organization, or person. Facebook pages are available to anyone on the Internet and are indexed by search engines such as Google. If a page isn't for yourself, you must have the legal right to create an official page for this business, organization, or brand. For example, if you own a small business, you have the right to create a Facebook page for your business. You can't, however, create a page for another business, product, or person you just happen to like.

A *Facebook profile* is for an individual to connect and share information with friends. You control the privacy rights and visibility of your profile as well as whom you connect with as a friend. You can post content only your friends can see—something you can't do with a page. For more information about creating a Facebook profile, see Chapter 2, "Setting Up Your Facebook Account and Profile."

If you're a public figure or solo business owner, you can create both a profile and page under your name. Use the page to connect with fans, supporters, and customers and the profile to connect with family members, friends, and colleagues.

A *Facebook group* enables you to create a community around any topic, such as a hobby or professional interest. For example, if you're an avid Adobe Photoshop user, you could create a group to share your expertise, but you couldn't create an official page unless you represent Adobe. Group options include open groups that anyone on Facebook can join, closed groups that require your approval to join, or secret groups that are hidden from Facebook group search results. For more information about creating a Facebook group, see Chapter 10, "Joining and Creating Groups."

Viewing a Facebook Page

Figure 14.1 shows an example of a Facebook page, one for Que Publishing.

Figure 14.1 *Promote a business or brand with a Facebook page.*

Although Facebook pages contain custom content, they all share the following elements, which are similar to a personal profile:

- A Wall for posting, liking, and commenting on status updates, links, photos, and videos.

- A photostrip at the top of your Wall with the five most recently posted or tagged photos.

- A series of links below the page logo that enable you to access other content. By default, every page includes a Wall and Info tab. Up to four other links also display. For additional content, click the More link.

TELL ME MORE   Media 14.1—Understanding Facebook Pages for Businesses and Brands
Access this audio recording through your registered Web Edition at my.safaribooksonline.com/9780132117029/media.

Searching for Facebook Pages

There are a variety of ways you can discover interesting Facebook pages. For example, you can

- Search for pages of interest by entering relevant keywords in the search box on the top of your Facebook screen

- Go to the Facebook Pages Directory (http://www.facebook.com/pages/?browse)

- View page suggestions that your friends share

- Visit websites and blogs you enjoy, which often promote their Facebook pages

LET ME TRY IT

Search for Facebook Pages by Keyword

To search for Facebook pages by keyword, follow these steps:

1. Enter keywords related to the topic you're searching for in the search box at the top of your Facebook screen.

2. Facebook displays the closest matches to your search term in a drop-down list. If you see the page you want, click its title to open it. If you don't see the page you want, click the See More Results link to display all results.

3. By default, Facebook displays all results for this search term, including people, pages, and groups. To narrow your results only to pages, click the Pages link on the left side of the page.

4. Your search results display each page's name and the number of Facebook members who like it. For example, Figure 14.2 displays sample search results for pages related to "Pearson Education." From this list, you can

   - Click the title of a page to view it directly.
   - Click the Like button to the right of the page name to "like" this page. For more information about what it means to like a page, see "Liking Facebook Pages" later in this chapter.

Figure 14.2   *Narrow down your results to find the right page.*

Participating on Facebook Pages

Because Facebook pages are customizable, there isn't one specific format for all pages. Pages do follow many of Facebook's standard conventions, however.

It's possible to perform many common Facebook tasks on a page, including

- Posting content on the page wall
- Commenting on, sharing, and liking other members' wall posts
- Viewing, commenting on, sharing, or tagging photos and videos
- Viewing and replying to discussion topics

Keep in mind that because each Facebook page is custom-designed, its content, format, and member privileges vary.

For a refresher on how to post wall content, photos, videos, events, and more, refer to the chapters in this book that focus on those topics.

 SHOW ME   Media 14.2—Exploring a Facebook Page
Access this video file through your registered Web Edition at
my.safaribooksonline.com/9780132117029/media.

Liking Facebook Pages

When you find a Facebook page you enjoy, show your support by liking it. As you're aware, you can like a variety of things on Facebook, including members' status updates, comments, photos, and videos. The capability to like extends to Facebook pages as well.

In addition to liking a page, you can also spread the word about pages by clicking the Share link at the bottom of the page's left column.

To like a Facebook page you're viewing, click the Like button to the right of its name, as shown in Figure 14.3. Be aware that if you've already liked this page, the Like button isn't available.

Figure 14.3   *When you like a page, its status updates display in your News Feed.*

You can also like a page by clicking the Like button to the right of a page's name in the search results that display after searching for a page.

When you like a page, Facebook posts this on your profile and adds this page to the list of liked pages at the bottom on your profile's Info tab (click the Show Other Pages link to display these).

Facebook lets you like only 500 pages. For most people, this is more than enough. If a Facebook page no longer interests you or you've reached your 500 page limit and need to make room for some new pages, you can unlike a page. To do so, scroll to the bottom of the page's left column and click the Unlike link (see Figure 14.4).

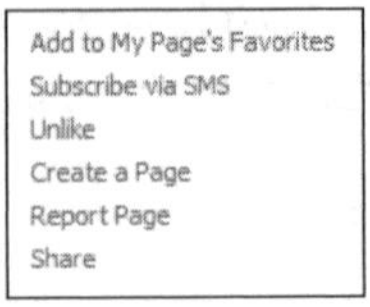

Add to My Page's Favorites
Subscribe via SMS
Unlike
Create a Page
Report Page
Share

Figure 14.4   *If you exceed the 500 page limit, you can unlike a page to make room for new interests.*

To return to Facebook pages you liked, you can

- View a list of your liked pages at the bottom of your profile's Info page.
- Go to the Facebook Pages Directory (www.facebook.com/pages/?browse) and click the My Pages link.

You can also keep up with your favorite pages by subscribing to receive updates by text message. To do so, click the Subscribe via SMS link on the page's left column. For more information about activating Facebook Mobile Texts, see Chapter 9, "Your Mobile Access to Facebook."

Creating Facebook Pages

If you run your own business or organization or are a public figure (author, speaker, musician, and so forth), you can create an official page to generate buzz and develop a community. Creating a Facebook page is straightforward. What's more difficult is determining exactly what to include on your page when you have so many options.

Planning Your Page

Before creating your page, you need to have a plan. First, take a look at a number of existing Facebook pages to get an idea of what's possible. Look at popular pages with a large number of fans, the pages of well-known companies and people in your industry, and your direct competitors' pages. As you do your research, consider the following questions:

- **What is the goal of your page?**—Do you want to use it to build community and awareness, find clients, sell products, or something else? Determining what you want to achieve by creating a Facebook page is critical to success.

- **What tabs do you want to include?**—Facebook pages include two default tabs: Wall and Info. You can also add one or more of Facebook's ready-made application tabs such as Photos or Video. Adding application tabs that display content from external sites such as your blog, YouTube, or Twitter is another option. A third option is to create custom tabs with unique content.

- **What tone do you want to convey?**—Is your page going to be conversational and encourage posting and participation from those who like it? Or is it more informational? Even if generating sales and improving your search engine optimization are primary goals, you should avoid a "direct sales" approach with your page. The best way to encourage visitors to like your page and return to it is to offer interesting, relevant content that educates, entertains, or informs them.

Creating Your Own Facebook Page

With your plan in place, it's time to create your Facebook page. Fortunately, with the up-front planning done, it's a quick process.

 SHOW ME   Media 14.3—Creating a Facebook Page
Access this video file through your registered Web Edition at
my.safaribooksonline.com/9780132117029/media.

 LET ME TRY IT

Create Your Own Facebook Page

To create your own Facebook page, follow these steps:

1. When logged in to Facebook, go to www.facebook.com/pages/create.php. Alternatively, click the Create a Page link at the bottom of the left column of any existing Facebook page.

You need a Facebook profile to create a Facebook page. If you don't have one, you can create both at the same time.

2. On the Create a Page page, click the box that best represents the page you want to create. Facebook replaces the box image with a series of fields that vary based on your selection, as shown in Figure 14.5. Your choices include

   - Local Business or Place
   - Company, Organization, or Institution
   - Brand or Product
   - Artist, Band, or Public Figure
   - Entertainment
   - Cause or Community

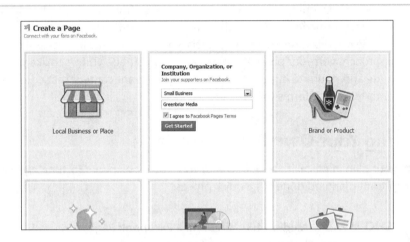

Figure 14.5   *Create an official page for yourself, your business, or your brand.*

3. Select the most appropriate category from the Choose a Category drop-down list. The options vary based on the page type you chose in step 2.

4. Enter your page name and any other required information for that page type. Remember that if you're creating an official page you must have the authority to create a page on Facebook. In other words, it's fine to create a page under your own name or business name, but you can't create a page using the name of another public figure or company you don't own or represent.

5. After reviewing Facebook's terms, click the I Agree to Facebook Pages Terms check box to confirm you understand and will comply with them.

6. Click the Get Started button. Facebook creates your page and opens the Get Started page where you can start editing its content.

You can edit your page at any time by navigating to its URL while you're logged into Facebook and clicking the Edit Page button in the upper-right corner.

Getting Started with Your Facebook Page

On the Get Started page, shown in Figure 14.6, Facebook prompts you to perform six tasks to help you get started on your new page.

Figure 14.6   *The Get Started page guides you in setting up your new Facebook page.*

These tasks include

- **Add an Image**—Personalize your page with your photo or company logo.
- **Invite Your Friends**—Suggest this Facebook page to your existing Facebook friends.
- **Tell Your Fans**—Notify current customer and email subscribers about your new Facebook page.
- **Post Status Updates**—Post a status update on your wall to start sharing information with others.

- **Promote This Page on Your Website**—Add a Facebook Like Box to your website or blog.

- **Set Up Your Mobile Phone**—Update your page via your mobile phone.

Remember that these are only suggestions. You can complete these tasks now, or finish them later. I recommend that you complete your page (add a picture, content, applications, and so forth) before telling others about your page or doing any promotion.

Personalizing Your Page with a Picture

Placing a picture or logo in the upper-left corner of your page helps to personalize it. Facebook also uses a thumbnail of this picture in other ways, such as next to any content you post on your Wall.

 LET ME TRY IT

Add a Picture to Your Page

To add a picture or logo to the upper-left corner of your page, follow these steps:

1. Pause your mouse over the large question mark in the upper-left corner of your page.

2. Click the Change Picture link.

3. On the Profile Picture section (see Figure 14.7), you can

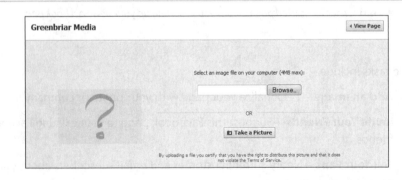

Figure 14.7   *Upload a picture or take one with your webcam.*

- Click the Browse button to select and upload a picture from your computer.

- Click the Take a Picture button to use your webcam to take and insert a picture.

Your picture now displays in the upper-left corner of your page, as shown in Figure 14.8.

Figure 14.8   *Personalize your page with a relevant photo or logo.*

You can edit your picture's thumbnail or delete it entirely by clicking the Change Picture link and selecting either Edit Thumbnail or Remove Your Picture from the menu.

The five most recent photos that you tag or post to your Wall display at the top of your page in a photostrip. To hide a photo, pause the mouse over it and click the Hide This Photo button (x). See Chapter 7, "Publishing Photos," to learn more about tagging photos.

Adding Information About Your Page

After personalizing your page with a picture or logo, you should add information about your page on its Info section. Clicking the Info tab is a common action when someone visits your Facebook page, so it pays to think carefully about what you enter here. Think of the keywords most relevant to your business and don't overload this section with unnecessary content.

LET ME TRY IT

Add Information About Your Page

To add information about your Facebook page, follow these steps:

1. Click the Info tab on your page's left column.

2. Click the Edit Info link to open the Basic Information section, shown in Figure 14.9.

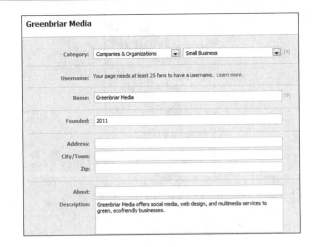

Figure 14.9 *Use relevant keywords in the Basic Information section.*

3. By default, this section displays the category, subcategory, and page name you entered when you created your page. Optionally, you can update these fields. Be aware that you can change your page name only if fewer than 100 people have liked your page.

If you've already secured your custom username, the Username field displays this name. If you haven't done this yet, you can click the Learn More link to do so if at least 25 people like your page. See "Creating a Custom Username" later in this chapter for more information.

4. Enter the appropriate data in the remaining fields on the Basic Information section. These fields vary based on the page type you selected when you

created the page. The fields on this page vary depending on the type of page you're creating, such as one for a local business, product, or public figure.

5. When you're finished, click the Save Changes button to display your new content (see Figure 14.10).

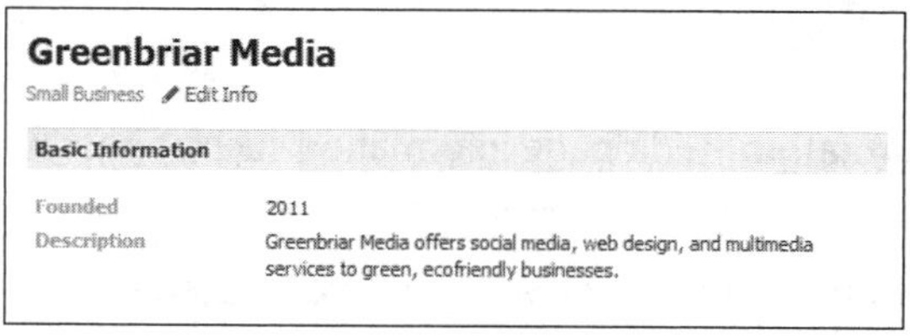

Greenbriar Media
Small Business   ✏ Edit Info

Basic Information

Founded   2011
Description   Greenbriar Media offers social media, web design, and multimedia
               services to green, ecofriendly businesses.

Figure 14.10   *Let your reader know about your business on the Info page.*

Customizing Your Page

To edit your page's settings, click the Edit Page button in the upper-right corner of your page. Figure 14.11 shows the available sections that enable you to customize the appearance and functionality of your Facebook page.

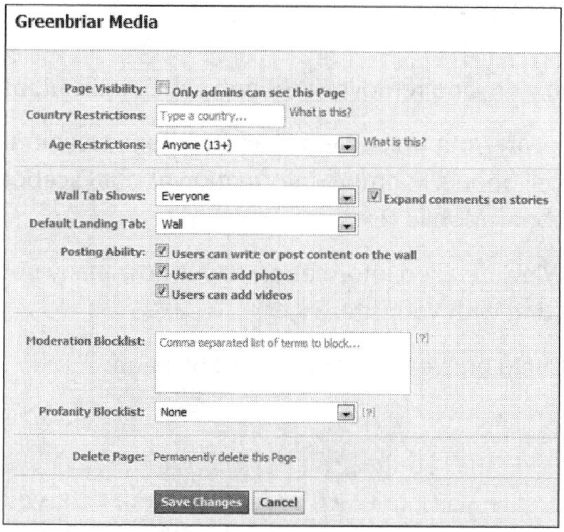

Greenbriar Media

Page Visibility: ☐ Only admins can see this Page
Country Restrictions: [Type a country...]   What is this?
Age Restrictions: [Anyone (13+) ▼]   What is this?

Wall Tab Shows: [Everyone ▼]   ☑ Expand comments on stories
Default Landing Tab: [Wall ▼]
Posting Ability: ☑ Users can write or post content on the wall
☑ Users can add photos
☑ Users can add videos

Moderation Blocklist: [Comma separated list of terms to block...]   [?]

Profanity Blocklist: [None ▼] [?]

Delete Page: Permanently delete this Page

[Save Changes] [Cancel]

Figure 14.11   *You can make extensive customizations to your Facebook page.*

- **Manage Permissions**—Specify any country or age restrictions for your page, what appears on your Wall, your default landing tab, users' posting ability, and any profanity blocklists you want to set (this helps prevent people from posting unwanted content on your Wall).

> If you're still working on your page, select the Only Admins Can See This Page checkbox to avoid showing it to the world before you're ready. When you finish your page, remove this checkmark.

- **Basic Information**—Edit page information such as your name, location, website, email, and company details.

- **Profile Picture**—Upload and edit your profile picture.

- **Featured**—Display other pages you like and user profiles of featured page owners.

- **Marketing**—Find links that enable you to advertise on Facebook, contact your fans, get a Facebook badge, or add a Like box to your website.

- **Manage Admins**—Add and remove page admins who have the right to manage your page.

> As the person who created this Facebook page, you're the only one with the rights to edit it. If you want to give administrator rights to another Facebook member as well, click Manage Admins.

- **Apps**—Add, edit, and remove Facebook page applications.

- **Mobile**—Locate your upload email address for uploading photos and videos from your cell phone. For more information about Facebook Mobile and activating Facebook Mobile Texts, see Chapter 9.

- **Insights**—View detailed information about how many people are viewing and interacting with your site.

- **Help**—Get help on creating your Facebook page.

> If you use an upload email address to upload photos and videos to your personal Facebook profile, you'll notice that Facebook provides you a different email address for use with your Facebook page. When accessing Facebook on a mobile device, it's important to distinguish whether you're updating your Facebook profile or your Facebook page.

Adding Applications to Your Facebook Page

The best way to enhance and customize your Facebook page is with Facebook applications. Fortunately, there are so many Facebook applications available that your biggest problem might only be choosing the right ones.

By default, Facebook makes the following applications available for your page: Events, Photos, Links, Notes, Video, and Discussion Boards. It's your choice whether you want to use any of these apps on your page. You can also browse for additional applications that might better suit your needs. The applications you add to your page display as tabs in the left column, just below your page logo. For example, in Figure 14.1 you can see that the Que Publishing page has the following application tabs: Offers, What's New, Series, and YouTube.

 SHOW ME   Media 14.4—Adding Applications to Your Facebook Page
Access this video file through your registered Web Edition at
my.safaribooksonline.com/9780132117029/media.

To add and manage Facebook applications for your page, click the Edit Page button on the upper-right corner of your page and then click the Apps tab. Figure 14.12 shows the available apps for your page.

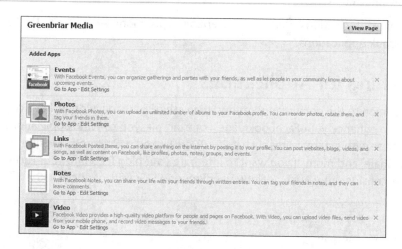

Figure 14.12   *Applications can enliven and personalize your Facebook page.*

Applications can include the following links:

- **Go to App**—Set up the application for your page. Because each application is unique, the setup steps vary by application.

- **Edit Settings**—Specify whether you want to display this application as its own tab. Figure 14.13 shows an example of the Edit Discussion Boards Settings dialog box.

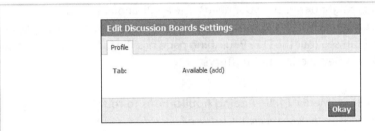

Figure 14.13   *Choose how you want to display your app on your Facebook page.*

To remove an application, click the Remove (x) button to its right. You can always add it back again by clicking the Browse More Applications link, searching for this application, and adding it.

For more information about using Facebook applications, see Chapter 13, "Using Facebook Applications."

Searching for Applications

In addition to the default applications, many third-party developers have created apps to enhance your Facebook page. For example, you can find applications that integrate with external sites such as YouTube, LinkedIn, Posterous, Eventbrite, SlideShare, and more. If you want to integrate your blog feed into your Facebook page, consider apps such as NetworkedBlogs, RSS Graffiti, or Social RSS.

You can also create your own custom tabs by using iFrame or by purchasing apps from companies such as TabSite (www.tabsite.com), North Social (www.northsocial.com), or Involver (www.involver.com).

LET ME TRY IT

Search for and Add Applications

To search for and add other applications, follow these steps:

1. Click the Edit Page button on the upper-right corner of your page.

2. In the left column, click the Apps tab.

3. Scroll down to the bottom of the page and click the Browse More Applications link.

4. On the All Apps page (see Figure 14.14), you can

   - Enter keywords in the search box to search for applications.

   - Browse applications by category by clicking the appropriate category link such as Business, Education, and so forth.

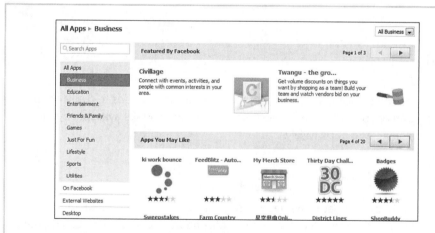

Figure 14.14 *Browse for the perfect application for your page.*

5. Review the search results to find the application you want and click its title. The application's Facebook page displays, as shown in Figure 14.15.

6. Click the Go To App button to complete the install process.

This application now displays in the Applications section where you can complete the setup necessary to add it to your page.

Figure 14.15   *Learn more about an app on its page.*

These steps describe the typical steps for adding new applications to your page. Because not every application works the same way, your actual steps might vary.

Remember that there is space for only a certain number of tabs to display on the left column of your page (six visible tabs, plus additional tabs available by clicking the More link). Add apps wisely.

Using Facebook as a Page

Using Facebook as a page enables you to post, like, and comment on other pages using your page name rather than your profile name. For example, let's say your name is Anne Smith and you created a page for your business, Waterfront Bistro. You can post, like, and comment as either yourself (Anne Smith) or as your business (Waterfront Bistro). This is a powerful promotional tool for your business, but be sure to add value and not over do it.

Figure 14.16 shows an example of a comment posted by a page rather than an individual.

To use Facebook as a page, you can

- Select Use Facebook as a Page from the Account drop-down menu on any Facebook screen and click the Switch button to the right of the page you want to use.

- Click the Use Facebook as [Page Name] link on the right side of the page you want to use.

Figure 14.16 *Gain name recognition for your business by using Facebook as a page.*

Promoting Your Facebook Page

Now that you've created a compelling, content-rich Facebook page, you need to get the word out about it. Here are several good ways to promote your page and get people to "like" it.

- **Secure a custom username**—Creating a short, memorable name that's easy for people to remember helps encourage page visitors. For more information, see "Creating a Custom Username" later in this section.

- **Add a Like Box to your website or blog**—For more information, see "Add a Like Box to Your Website or Blog" later in this section.

- **Invite your friends to your Facebook page**—To do so, click the Suggest to Friends link on the right side of your page's, select the friends you want to invite, and click the Send Recommendations button.

- **Share information about your page to your profile**—To do so, click the Share link at the bottom of your page's left column. Enter any comments in the dialog box and then click the Share button.

- **Promote your page with an ad**—Click the Promote with an Ad link on the right side of your page to create your ad. Remember that there are costs associated with advertising on Facebook.

- **Share on the social web**—Spread the news about your new page with your audience on other social sites such as Twitter, LinkedIn, and others.

- **Share with your subscribers**—If you publish an ezine, be sure to include a link to your Facebook page in every issue.

> To keep tabs on the success of your promotional efforts, click the View Insights link on the right side your page. You can view your monthly active users, daily new likes, daily post views, and daily post feedback.

Creating a Custom Username

If at least 25 people like your Facebook page, you can secure a custom username for it. For example, when you first create your page, Facebook could assign you a URL like this: http://www.facebook.com/pages/Patrice-Anne-Rutledge/143355035682739. A custom username enables you to create a shorter, more memorable URL for your page, such as http://www.facebook.com/AuthorPatriceRutledge, that you can promote on your website, blog, or business card.

 LET ME TRY IT

Create a Custom Username for Your Page

To create a custom username for your page, follow these steps:

1. When logged in to Facebook, go to www.facebook.com/username.

2. Select your page from the Page Name drop-down list and enter your desired username (see Figure 14.17). Try to create a username that closely matches your official identity or business name. Usernames can contain only alphanumeric characters (such as A-Z or 0-9) or a period.

Figure 14.17   *Enter a permanent username for your Facebook page.*

You can't change your username, so consider carefully before choosing a name and verify there are no typos!

3. Click the Check Availability button. If your username is available, the User-name Available dialog box opens. If it isn't available, try another username.

4. Click the Confirm button to permanently set your username.

5. The Success dialog box opens, letting you know that your new username is official. Click the Okay button to close this dialog box.

Promoting Your Page with a Like Box

A Like Box is a widget that you can place on an external website or blog, letting everyone know about your Facebook page.

 LET ME TRY IT

Add a Like Box to Your Website or Blog

If you want to add a Like Box to your website or blog, follow these steps:

1. Click the Edit Page button in the upper-right corner of your page.

2. Click the Marketing tab.

3. Click the Add a Like Box to Your Website link. Figure 14.18 shows the Like Box page where you can customize your Like Box.

4. Enter your page's URL in the Facebook Page URL field. For example, http://www.facebook.com/AuthorPatriceRutledge.

5. The remainder of the page displays Facebook's default settings for Like Boxes. You can accept Facebook's defaults or modify any of the following settings:

   • **Width**—If you're placing this box in a narrow sidebar, enter the appropriate width in pixels.

   • **Color Scheme**—You can choose either a light or dark color scheme, which blends best with the website you're adding the Like Box to.

   • **Show Faces**—By default, Facebook displays profile photos of random fans. If you don't want to display these photos, remove the checkmark.

- **Stream**—Select whether you want to display your latest page status updates.
- **Header**—Select this check box if you want to display your page's header.

Figure 14.18 *Customize the size and appearance of your Like Box.*

6. Click the Get Code button when you're done. The Your Like Box Plugin Code dialog box opens, shown in Figure 14.19.

7. Copy the text in the iframe section and paste this HTML into an appropriate location on your site. Your blog's sidebar is a great place to include a Like Box.

8. Click the Okay button to close the dialog box.

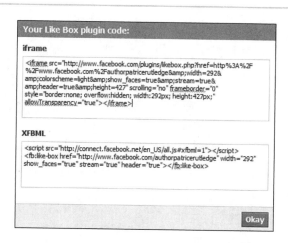

Figure 14.19 *Copy your code and paste into your website or blog.*

index